CURRENT ISSUE AND SOCIETAL DEVELOPMENT

FOR BBA (3RD SEMESTER) OF BHAGAT PHOOL SINGH WOMEN'S UNIVERSITY, KHANPUR

ANNU SEHRAWAT

ISBN 979-888546637-0

THE CONSTITUTION OF INDIA

PREAMBLE

WE, THE PEOPLE OF INDIA, having solemnly resolved to constitute India into a SOVEREIGN SOCIALIST SECULAR DEMOCRATIC REPUBLIC and to secure to all its citizens:

JUSTICE, social, economic and political;

LIBERTY of thought, expression, belief, faith and worship;

EQUALITY of status and of opportunity; and to promote among them all

FRATERNITY assuring the dignity of the individual and the unity and integrity of the Nation;

WE DO HEREBY GIVE TO OURSELVES THIS CONSTITUTION.

Contents

Foreword

BPS University, Khanpur has revised the cousre contents of BBA Course. This book has been especially written for the new syllabus of **Paper Code : BBL - 114** "Current Issue and Societal DevDevelopment". Some of the Distinguishing featuresof the book are as follows :

- Full Coverage of the prescribed syllabus.
- Systematic and sequential arrangement of topics as per the syllabus.
- Lucid and simple language.

I am sure that this book would be very useful both studentsand teachers. Suggestions and critical comments for improvementof the book are welcome.

E- Mail : annusehrawat8520@gmail.com
Website : annusehrawat8520.blogspot.com
Author

Preface

First credit is given, my teachers "**Dr. Prashant Kumar**" and "**Mr. Kapil**" have given full cooperation in this work. Respected Principal Sir "**Mr. Dinesh Singh**" gave full cooperation in moving forward.

Second credit, I want to give to **my parents** who took good upbringing of me and always keep inspiring me to move forward in life.

Author

Prologue

SYLLABUS

BPS UNIVERSITY, KHANPUR

B.B.A. (3rd Semester)

Current issue and Societal Development

Paper Code : BBL - 114

UNIT -1

- Law related to hindu marriage
- Dowry
- Sexual Harassment of Women
- Consumer protection Act 1986

UNIT - 2

- Fundamentals rights of citizens
- Right in relation to police
- RTI
- Lokayukt
- RTE Act - 2009

UNIT - 3

- Property Rights
- Human rights
- Right to maintenance
- Motor Vehicle claim Tribunals

UNIT - 4

- Environment and Pollution

- Labour Law

CHAPTER ONE

Hindu Marriage Act, 1955

The Hindu Marriage Act, 1955 was intended to secure the rights of marriage for the bride and groom who are Hindu and are bound under the sacred bond of marriage under any ceremony. The law does not define the kind of ceremony since there are several ways a man and a woman may carry out this religious act. This act was floated after several cases were seen where both man and woman were petrified or humiliated under a fraud case in the name of marriage. This act is binding to any person who is Hindu, Jain, Sikh and Buddhists and is not a Muslim, Christian, Parsi or Jew and is governed by some other law. This law is binding to any person who is Hindu by Birth or Hindu by Religion. There is a complete definition of Hindu under Section 2 of Hindu Marriage Act.

This law was enacted to avoid the various consequences which were prevalent due to immature Hindu law for marriage under British Rule.

Below are some important components to make you aware of this Hindu Marriage law:

- **Section 5 of Hindu Marriage Act, 1955:**

As per Section 5(ii) and (iii) of Hindu Marriage Act, 1955, the Hindu marriage is not so much of a religion and is more of a result of mutual consent.

- **Section 2 of Hindu Marriage Act, 1955 :**

As per Section 2 of Hindu Marriage Act, 1955, marriage amongst Hindus in any form irrespective of caste or creed or amongst any person who is bound under Hindu Marriage Act, 1955 like Buddhists, Sikhs, Jains and so called Hindus is a Hindu Marriage.

- **Section 3 of Hindu Marriage Act, 1955:**

Section 3 of Hindu Marriage Act, 1955 revoked the prohibited degrees of relationships which was defined in Smritis and have defined certain new prohibited degree of relationships e.g. A person cannot marry his brother's wife. However, this provision shall not apply in case of divorcee and widow women.

- **Provisions under Section 5 and Section 17 of Hindu Marriage Act:**

Hindu Marriage Act, 1955 incorporated Monogamy and strictly prohibits a Hindu from getting involved in a marital relationship with more than one person. Bigamy and Polygamy, if proved is strictly punishable under the Indian Penal Code as per provisions under Section 5 and Section 17 of Hindu Marriage Act, 1955. • There are no restrictions imposed under the Hindu Marriage Act, 1955 in terms of caste and communities. Hence Inter-caste and inter-communal marriages are completely lawful under this act.

• Hindu Marriage Act, 1955 removed any distinction under law of a marriage of a maiden and a widow and both are treated equally under this law. • Section 5 of Hindu Marriage Act, 1955 makes a marriage lawful only if the groom has attained the age of 21 years at the time of marriage and bride has attained the age of 18 years at the time of marriage. • Section 5 defines various conditions when a marriage is considered valid under the Hindu Marriage Act, 1955.

- **Section 8 of the Hindu Marriage Act, 1955:**

Section 8 of Hindu Marriage Act, 1955 have introduced the provision of registering the marriage under this Act.

- **Section 9 of the Hindu Marriage Act:**

Section 9 of Hindu Marriage Act, 1955 defined the restitution of conjugal rights of husband and wife, bound under this Act.

- **Section 15 of Hindu Marriage Act:**

Section 15 of Hindu Marriage Act, 1955 states that after a valid divorce either party is eligible to re-marry.

- **Section 6 of Marriage Act, 1955:**

Section 16 of Hindu Marriage Act, 1955 defines the legitimacy of children born out the alliance and can be subsequently declared annulled or void or voidable.

- **Section 24 of Hindu Act, 1955:**

Section 24 of Hindu Marriage Act, 1955 defines the provision of maintenance pendent lite and for expenses of legal proceedings of a divorce.

- **Hindu Marriage Act Section 25:**

Section 25 of Hindu Marriage Act, 1955 defines complete provision of permanent alimony and maintenance for the alliances under this Act.

- **Section 26 of Hindu Marriage Act, 1955:**

Section 26 of Hindu Marriage Act, 1955 defines the provisions for custody, maintenance, and education of minor children during and after legal proceedings of divorce.

Conditions of Valid marriage

The Hindu marriage Act 1955 has provided five conditions as pre-requisites for valid Hindu marriage, under section 5 of Act.

Section 5[1] provides that a marriage can be solemnised between two Hindus, if the following conditions are fulfilled:

1. Spouse living at time of the marriage: neither of the parties to marriage should have any spouse living at the time of marriage.
2. At time of marriage, neither party to marriage should be incapable of giving a valid consent for the marriage.

3. At the time of marriage, though capable of giving a valid consent, is suffering from any mental disorder of any such type or to such extent, that is unfit for marriage or procreating children.
4. At the time of marriage, has been subject to recurring attacks of insanity.
5. Age of the bridegroom and bride must be 21 and 18 years of age, respectively.
6. The parties must not be within the degrees of the prohibited relationship. Exception to this is only provided if the custom or usage governing them, allows such a marriage.
7. The parties must not be sapindas of each other. Exception to this is provided by the permission of customs or usages governing the parties.

DESCRIPTION OF CONDITIONS

Following are the conditions required to be fulfilled for a valid Hindu marriage:

1. **MONOGAMY:**

Hindu Marriage Act, 1955 provides the rule of monogamy & prohibits polygamy & polyandry. A Hindu before this law could marry any number of wives , even if he had a wife or wives living, although this practice was looked always with disfavour. When a wife has more than one husband at one time this is called polyandry. From the ancient times to 1955, polygamy was recognised in Hindu Law, but polyandry was never permitted . Section 17[2] would render the offending party liable for prosecution under section 494 and 495 of IPC ,1860. A second marriage in the lifetime of a spouse of first marriage, will be against law and considered void even if second marriage were contracted outside India. In order to prosecute a person for bigamy it is necessary to prove that he/she already has a living spouse & prior marriage has been duly celebrated with the performance of ceremonies.

2. SANITY OR MENTAL CAPACITY:

Section 5(ii) provides about the mental capacity of the spouses at the time of marriage. It was provided, in the original act, that neither party to a marriage should be idiot or lunatic at the time of marriage. The marriage laws amendment Act 1976 framed the clause & explained insanity or mental disorder.

This clause provides : "at the time of marriage neither party should be incapable of giving valid consent to it in consequences of unsoundness of mind; or though capable of giving the valid consent , has been suffering from mental disorder of such kind or kind to such extent as to be unfit for marriage & procreation of children; or has been subject to recurrent attack of insanity or epilepsy.

Thus, the mental incapacity of any form, affecting the very purpose of marriage has been ground of voidability of marriage. The mental disorder of insanity must be in existence at the time of marriage. Such marriages may be declared as voidable under section 12 of the act[3] . But if a person subsequent to the date of marriage suffers from mental disorder or insanity ,the provision of this clause are not contravened, because it applies to such case where the parties are insane at the time of marriage.

3. AGE OF PARTIES TO MARRIAGE:

The minimum age for marriage is fixed. According to the Hindu Marriage act 1955, the age provided for the groom was 18 years & for the bride 15 years. Though where the age of a bride was below 18, the consent of her guardian was necessary. Now, the child Marriage Restrain (Amendment)Act, 1978, has revised the minimum age fixed for marriage to 21 years in case of groom & 18yrs of age in case of bride. A contravention of this clause would neither render the marriage void under section 11 of this act nor voidable under section 12 of the act. The Hindu Marriage Act provides in section 18 punishment of child marriage i.e., imprisonment upto 15 days or a fine upto Rs 1000 or both).

4. BEYOND PROHIBITED DEGREE:

Section 5(iv) prohibits marriage between the person who are within the "prohibited degree of relationship with each other". Section 3(g) provides," two person are said to be within the degree prohibited relationship:

i. If one is lineal ascendant of the other; or

ii. If one was the wife or husband of lineal ascendant or descendant of the other; or

iii. If one was the wife of the brother or of the father's or mother's brother or of the grandfather's or grandmother's brother of the other; or

iv. If the two are brother-and-sister, uncle-and-niece, aunt-and-nephew, or children of brother and sister or of two brother and sister or of two brothers or sisters.

It should also be noted that prohibited relationship includes –

i. Relationship by half or uterine blood as well as by full blood,

ii. Illegitimate blood relationship as well as legitimate,

iii. Relationship by adoption as well as by blood; and all of terms of relationship in those clauses shall be construed accordingly. But if the custom or usage governing each of parties to the marriage allows the marriage within the degree of prohibited relationship, then such marriage will be valid & binding.

5. BEYOND SAPINDA RELATIONSHIP:

Section 5(v) prohibits marriage between persons who are sapindas of each other. A marriage in contravention of this clause, .i.e., it will be void & may be so declared under section 11 and the person contravening to the provision of this clause would be punishable under section 18. The word "sapinda" means relation connected through same body.

According to section 3(f) Sapinda relationship defined:

i. "sapinda relationship" with reference to any person extends as far as the 3rd generation (inclusive) in the line of ascent through the mother, and 5th generation (inclusive) in the line of ascent through father, the line being traced upwards in each case from the person concerned, who is to be counted as the first generation.

ii. Two persons are said to be "sapindas" of each other if one is lineal ascendant of other within the limits of sapinda relationship within the limits of sapinda relationship with reference each of them.

CONCLUSION

A marriage under Hindu law is a sacrament that requires the above-mentioned conditions of marriage. Thus, in order to constitute a valid Hindu marriage under Hindu law, parties to marriage should be monogamous, should have sound mind, should be major by age and should be beyond prohibited degree. A marriage fulfilling these conditions is considered to be valid and have effect under the Hindu Marriage Act, 1955.

[1]Hindu Marriage Act, 1985

[2] Section 17 of Hindu Marriage Act, 1985

[3]Hindu Marriage Act, 1955

CHAPTER TWO

PROHIBITED DEGREE

Conditions of a Hindu Marriage

A marriage to be valid has to fulfill the following conditions:

- Neither party should have a spouse living at the time of marriage. The spouse does not include a divorced husband/ wife.
- At the time of marriage, the parties should be capable of giving a valid consent to the marriage. A person who is of a sound mind shall be considered to be a person capable to give a valid consent. Neither party, though capable of giving a valid consent should be suffering from mental disorder of such a kind or to such an extent as to be unfit for marriage and procreation of children. Neither party should be suffering from recurrent attacks of insanity or epilepsy.
- The bridegroom should have attained the age of 21 years and the bride should have attained the age of 18 years at the time of marriage.
- The parties should not be within the degrees of prohibited relationships, unless the customs or usage, permits such a marriage.

Two persons are said to be within the degrees of prohibited relationships:

- if one is a lineal ascendant of the other. For example a Daughter can not marry her father and grandfather. Similarly, a mother can not marry her son or grandson.
- If one was the wife or husband of a lineal ascendant or descendant of the other. For example, a son can not marry his stepmother. Similarly, a person can not marry his Daughter-in -Law or son -in-law.
- If one was the wife of the brother or of the father's or mother's brother or the grandfather's or grandmother's brother of the other.
- If the two are brother and sister; uncle and niece; Aunt and Nephew or children of brother and sister of two brothers or two sisters. It must have been noticed in some communities the marriage with the wife of the brother and mother's brother and the first cousins are solemnized, those marriages, in the absence of a custom in the community are not valid marriages.

The parties are not apindas of each other, unless the customs or usage governing each of them permits of a marriage between the two. A apindas relationship with reference to any person extends as far as the third generation (inclusive) in the line of ascent through the mother, and the fifth (inclusive) in the line of ascent through the father.

In plain words, a person can not marry up to his second cousin from the mother's side and up to his fourth cousin from the side of the father. It is also necessary the parties should not be apindas of each other from either side.

In case, either party has a spouse living at the time of marriage, within the degree of prohibited relationship and are apindas of each other, the marriage between the parties shall be null and void.

CHAPTER THREE

GROUNDS OF DIVORCE

Grounds for divorce in India:

The secular mindset of the Indian judicial system has initiated the proclamation of various personal laws based on different religious faiths. Hindus, Christians, and Muslims are governed under separate marriage acts and grounds for divorce in India.

Grounds for Divorce under the Hindu Marriage Act, 1955

The following are the grounds for divorce in India mentioned under the Hindu Marriage Act, 1955.

1. Adultery –

The act of indulging in any kind of sexual relationship including intercourse outside marriage is termed adultery. Adultery is counted as a criminal offense and substantial proof are required to establish it. An amendment to the law in 1976 states that one single act of adultery is enough for the petitioner to get a divorce.

2. Cruelty –

A spouse can file a divorce case when he/she is subjected to any kind of mental and physical injury that causes danger to life, limb and health. The intangible acts of cruelty through mental torture are not judged upon one single act but series of incidents. Certain instances like the food being denied, continuous ill-treatment and abuses to acquire dowry, perverse sexual act etc are included under cruelty.

3. Desertion –

If one of the spouses voluntarily abandons his/her partner for at least a period of two years, the abandoned spouse can file a divorce case on the ground of desertion.

4. Conversion –

In case either of the two converts himself/herself into another religion, the other spouse may file a divorce case based on this ground.

5. Mental Disorder –

Mental disorder can become a ground for filing a divorce if the spouse of the petitioner suffers from incurable mental disorder and insanity and therefore cannot be expected from the couple to stay together.

6. Leprosy –

In case of a 'virulent and incurable' form of leprosy, a petition can be filed by the other spouse based on this ground.

7. Venereal Disease –

If one of the spouses is suffering from a serious disease that is easily communicable, a divorce can be filed by the other spouse. Sexually transmitted diseases like AIDS are accounted to be venereal diseases.

8. Renunciation –

A spouse is entitled to file for a divorce if the other renounces all worldly affairs by embracing a religious order.

9. Not Heard Alive –

If a person is not seen or heard alive by those who are expected to be 'naturally heard' of the person for a continuous period of seven years, the person is presumed to be dead. The other spouse should need to file a divorce if he/she is interested in remarriage.

10. No Resumption of Co-habitation –

It becomes a ground for divorce if the couple fails to resume their co-habitation after the court has passed a decree of separation.

The following are the grounds for divorce in India on which a petition can be filed only by the wife.

1) If the husband has indulged in rape, bestiality and sodomy.

2) If the marriage is solemnized before the Hindu Marriage Act and the husband has again married another woman in spite of the first wife being alive, the first wife can seek for a divorce.

3) A girl is entitled to file for a divorce if she was married before the age of fifteen and renounces the marriage before she attains eighteen years of age.

4) If there is no co-habitation for one year and the husband neglects the judgment of maintenance awarded to the wife by the court, the wife can contest for a divorce.

The following are the grounds of divorce mentioned under the Indian Divorce Act, 1869.

1) Adultery

2) Conversion to another religion

3) One of the couples suffering from an unsound mind, leprosy or communicable venereal disease for at least two years before the filing of the divorce.

4) Not been seen or heard alive for a period of seven or more years.

5) Failure in observing the restitution of conjugal rights for at least two years.

6) Inflicting cruelty and giving rise to mental anxiety that can be injurious to health and life.

7) Wife can file a divorce based on the grounds of rape, sodomy and bestiality.

RIGHTS OF WIFE

The Constitution has provided many rights to the wife. Some of the key rights are:

1. Right to Streedhan:

Streedhan is the property which a woman obtains at the time of her marriage, it is different from the Dowry in a way that it is voluntarily gifts given to the wife before or after her marriage and there is no element of coercion. The Courts have clearly said that women will have absolute rights over their streedhan even if it is placed in the custody of her husband or in-laws. The case of Pratibha Rani vs. Suraj Kumar1 also discussed.

2. Right to residence:

A wife has the absolute right to reside in a matrimonial household where his husband resides, irrespective of whether it is an ancestral house, a joint family home, a self-acquired home or a rental house.

3. Right to a committed relationship:

A Hindu male is bound not to marry any other girl or have an affair with anyone else unless he is legally divorced. In case if the husband having a relationship with any other woman then he will be charged of adultery under section 497 of IPC. His wife has the right to file divorce on the ground of having an extra-marital relationship with any other woman.

4. Right to maintenance by husband:

Under section 18 of the Hindu Adoption and Maintenance Act, 1956 a Hindu wife is entitled to claim maintenance from her husband in case if he is guilty of cruelty, desertion, polygamy or has a venereal disease, thereby enforcing her rights in divorce. Under section 25 of this act provides for permanent Alimony and Maintenance. This section allows any court which has jurisdiction under this Act may pass an order upon receiving an application from the aggrieved spouse directing the respondent to pay the applicant for her support and maintenance.

5. Right to live with dignity and self-respect:

A wife has the right to live her life with dignity and to have the same lifestyle that of her husband and in-laws have. She also has right to live free from any mental or physical torture.

6. Right to child maintenance:

Husband and wife must provide for their minor child. If the wife is incapable of earning, then the husband must provide her financial support.

CHAPTER FOUR

DOWRY

dowry, the money, goods, or estate that a woman brings to her husband or his family in marriage. Most common in cultures that are strongly patrilineal and that expect women to reside with or near their husband's family (patrilocality), dowries have a long history in Europe, South Asia, Africa, and other parts of the world.

One of the basic functions of a dowry has been to serve as a form of protection for the wife against the very real possibility of ill treatment by her husband and his family. A dowry used in this way is actually a conditional gift that is supposed to be restored to the wife or her family if the husband divorces, abuses, or commits other grave offenses against her. Land and precious metals have often been used in this form of dowry and are frequently inalienable by the husband, though he might otherwise use and profit from them during the marriage.

A dowry sometimes serves to help a new husband discharge the responsibilities that go with marriage. This function assumes special importance in societies where marriages have regularly been made between very young people; the dowry enables the new couple to establish a household, which they otherwise would not have been able to do. In some societies a dowry provides the wife with a means of support in case of her husband's death. In this latter case the dowry may be seen as a substitute for her inheritance of all or part of her husband's estate.

In many societies, dowries have served as a reciprocal gesture by the bride's kin to the groom's kin for the expenses incurred by the latter in payment of bridewealth. These exchanges are not purely economic but instead serve to ratify the marriage and consolidate friendship between the two families.

In medieval and Renaissance Europe, the dowry frequently served not only to enhance the desirability of a woman for marriage but also to build the power and wealth of great families and even to determine the frontiers and policies of states. The use of dowries more or less disappeared in Europe in the 19th and 20th centuries. In some other places, however, dowries grew in popularity at the end of the 20th century, even when declared illegal or otherwise discouraged by governments. In South Asia, for instance, parents of the groom have sometimes demanded compensation for their son's higher education and future earnings, which the bride would ostensibly share.

Dowry Prohibition Act India [1961]

Dowry Prohibition Act, Indian law, enacted on May 1, 1961, intended to prevent the giving or receiving of a dowry. Under the Dowry Prohibition Act, dowry includes property, goods, or money given by either party to the marriage, by the parents of either party, or by anyone else in connection with the marriage. The Dowry Prohibition Act applies to persons of all religions in India.

The original text of the Dowry Prohibition Act was widely judged to be ineffective in curbing the practice of dowry. Moreover, specific forms of violence against women continued to be linked to a failure to meet dowry demands. As a result, the legislation underwent subsequent amendment. In 1984, for example, it was changed to specify that presents given to a bride or a groom at the time of a wedding are allowed. The law required, however, that a list be maintained describing each gift, its value, the identity of the person giving it, and the person's relation to either party to the marriage. The act and relevant sections of the Indian Penal Code were further amended to protect female victims of dowry-related violence. Another layer of legal protection was provided in 2005 under the Protection of Women from Domestic Violence Act.

Amendments to the original Dowry Prohibition Act also established minimum and maximum punishments for giving and receiving dowry and created a penalty for demanding dowry or advertising offers of money or property in connection with a marriage. The Indian Penal Code was also modified in 1983 to establish specific crimes of dowry-related cruelty, dowry death, and abetment of suicide. These enactments punished violence against women by their husbands or their relatives when proof of dowry demands or dowry harassment could be shown.

Despite the revisions, however, the practice of dowry and dowry-related violence still occurs in varying degrees within several communities and socioeconomic groups of India.

CHAPTER FIVE

Sexual Harassment

The EEOC has defined sexual harassment in its guidelines as:

Unwelcome sexual advances, requests for sexual favors, and other verbal or physical
conduct of a sexual nature when:

- Submission to such conduct is made either explicitly or implicitly a term or condition of an individual's employment, or
- Submission to or rejection of such conduct by an individual is used as a basis for employment decisions affecting such individual, or
- Such conduct has the purpose or effect of unreasonably interfering with an individual's work performance or creating an intimidating, hostile, or offensive working environment.

Unwelcome Behavior is the critical word. Unwelcome does not mean "involuntary."

A victim may consent or agree to certain conduct and actively participate in it even though it is offensive and objectionable. Therefore, sexual conduct is unwelcome whenever the person subjected to it considers it unwelcome. Whether the person in fact welcomed a request for a date, sex-oriented comment, or joke depends on all the circumstances.

Source: Preventing Sexual Harassment (BNA Communications, Inc.) SDC IP .73

1992 manual

Sexual harassment includes many things...

- Actual or attempted rape or sexual assault.
- Unwanted pressure for sexual favors.
- Unwanted deliberate touching, leaning over, cornering, or pinching.
- Unwanted sexual looks or gestures.
- Unwanted letters, telephone calls, or materials of a sexual nature.
- Unwanted pressure for dates.
- Unwanted sexual teasing, jokes, remarks, or questions.
- Referring to an adult as a girl, hunk, doll, babe, or honey.
- Whistling at someone.
- Cat calls.
- Sexual comments.
- Turning work discussions to sexual topics.
- Sexual innuendos or stories.
- Asking about sexual fantasies, preferences, or history.
- Personal questions about social or sexual life.
- Sexual comments about a person's clothing, anatomy, or looks.
- Kissing sounds, howling, and smacking lips.

- Telling lies or spreading rumors about a person's personal sex life.
- Neck massage.
- Touching an employee's clothing, hair, or body.
- Giving personal gifts.
- Hanging around a person.
- Hugging, kissing, patting, or stroking.
- Touching or rubbing oneself sexually around another person.
- Standing close or brushing up against a person.
- Looking a person up and down (elevator eyes).
- Staring at someone.
- Sexually suggestive signals.
- Facial expressions, winking, throwing kisses, or licking lips.
- Making sexual gestures with hands or through body movements.

Examples

VERBAL

- Referring to an adult as a girl, hunk, doll, babe, or honey
  - Whistling at someone, cat calls
  - Making sexual comments about a person's body
  - Making sexual comments or innuendos
  - Turning work discussions to sexual topics
  - Telling sexual jokes or stories
  - Asking about sexual fantasies, preferences, or history
  - Asking personal questions about social or sexual life
  - Making kissing sounds, howling, and smacking lips

· Making sexual comments about a person's clothing, anatomy, or looks

· Repeatedly asking out a person who is not interested

· Telling lies or spreading rumors about a person's personal sex life

NON-VERBAL

· Looking a person up and down (Elevator eyes)

· Staring at someone

· Blocking a person's path

· Following the person

· Giving personal gifts

· Displaying sexually suggestive visuals

· Making sexual gestures with hands or through body movements

· Making facial expressions such as winking, throwing kisses, or licking lips

PHYSICAL

· Giving a massage around the neck or shoulders

· Touching the person's clothing, hair, or body

· Hugging, kissing, patting, or stroking

· Touching or rubbing oneself sexually around another person

· Standing close or brushing up against another person

Terminology

SEXISM is an attitude. It is an attitude of a person of one sex that he or she is superior to a person of the other sex.

For example, a man thinks that women are too emotional. Or a woman thinks that men are chauvinists.

SEX DISCRIMINATION *is a behavior. It occurs when employment decisions are based on an employees sex or when an employee is treated differently because of his or her sex. For example, a female supervisor always asks the male employees, in a coed workplace, to move the boxes of computer paper. Or, a male supervisor always asks the female employees, in a coed workplace to plan office parties.*

SEXUAL HARASSMENT *is a behavior. It is defined as unwelcome behavior of a sexual nature. For example, a man whistles at a woman when she walks by. Or a woman looks a man up and down when he walks towards her.*

SUBTLE SEXUAL HARASSMENT *is a behavior but not a legal term. It is unwelcome behavior of a sexual nature that if allowed to continue could create a QUID PRO QUO and/or a Hostile Work Environment for the recipient. For example, unwelcome sexual comments, jokes, innuendoes.*

QUID PRO QUO HARASSMENT *is when employment and/or employment decisions for an employee are based on that employees's* *acceptance or rejection of unwelcome sexual behavior. For example, a supervisor fires an employee because that employee will not go out with him or her.*

HOSTILE WORK ENVIRONMENT *is a work environment created by unwelcome sexual behavior or behavior directed at an employee because of that employee's sex that is offensive, hostile and/or intimidating and that adversely affects that employee's ability to do his or her job. For example, pervasive unwelcome sexual comments or jokes that continue*

QUID PRO QUO HARASSMENT *is when employment and/or employment decisions for an employee are based on that employees's acceptance or rejection of unwelcome sexual behavior. For example, a supervisor fires an employee because that employee will not go out with him or her.*

HOSTILE WORK ENVIRONMENT *is a work environment created by unwelcome sexual behavior or behavior directed at an employee because of that employee's sex that is offensive, hostile and/or intimidating and that adversely affects that employee's ability to do his or her job.*

For example, pervasive unwelcome sexual comments or jokes that continue even though the recipient has indicated that those behaviors are unwelcome.

CHAPTER SIX

Vishakha and others v State of Rajasthan

In India, before 1997, there were no formal guidelines for how an incident involving sexual harassment at workplace should be dealt by an employer. Women experiencing sexual harassment at workplace had to lodge a complaint under Section 354 of the Indian Penal Code that deals with the 'criminal assault of women to outrage women's modesty' and Section 509 that punishes an individual or individuals for using a 'word, gesture or act intended to insult the modesty of a woman'. These sections left the interpretation of 'outraging women's modesty' to the discretion of the police officer.

During the 1990s, Rajasthan state government employee Bhanwari Devi who tried to prevent child marriage as part of her duties as a worker of the Women Development Programme was raped by the landlords of the gujjar community. The feudal patriarchs who were enraged by her (in their words: "a lowly woman from a poor and potter community") 'guts' decided to teach her a lesson and raped her repeatedly.[6] The rape survivor did not get justice from Rajasthan High Court and the rapists were allowed to go free. This inspired several women's groups and NGOs to file a petition in the Supreme Court under the collective platform of Vishaka.

This case brought to the attention of the Supreme Court of India, "the absence of domestic law occupying the field, to formulate effective measures to check the evil of sexual harassment of working women at all work places."

Judgement

In 1997, the Supreme Court delivered a landmark judgment laying down guidelines to be followed by establishments in dealing with complaints about sexual harassment. "Vishaka Guidelines" were stipulated by the Supreme Court of India, in Vishaka and others v State of Rajasthan case in 1997, regarding sexual harassment at workplace. The court stated that these guidelines were to be implemented until legislation is passed to deal with the issue.

The court decided that the consideration of "International Conventions and norms are significant for the purpose of interpretation of the guarantee of gender equality, right to work with human dignity in Articles 14, 15 19(1)(g) and 21 of the Constitution and the safeguards against sexual harassment implicit therein."

The court also defined sexual harassment as including such unwelcome sexually determined behaviour (whether directly or by implication) like physical contact and advances, a demand or request for sexual favours, sexually coloured remarks, showing pornography, or any other unwelcome physical verbal or non-verbal conduct of sexual nature. The court recognised that where any of these acts is committed in circumstances where under the victim of such conduct has a reasonable apprehension that in relation to the victim's employment or work whether she is drawing salary, or honorarium or voluntary, whether in government, public or private enterprise such conduct can be humiliating and may constitute a health and safety problem. The court noted that it was discriminatory when the woman has reasonable grounds to believe that objecting to sexual harassment would disadvantage her in connection with her employment or work including recruiting or promotion or when it creates a hostile work environment. Thus, sexual harassment need not involve physical contact. Any act that creates a hostile work environment — be it by virtue of cracking lewd jokes, verbal abuse, circulating lewd rumours etc. — counts as sexual harassment.[8] The creation of a hostile work environment through unwelcome physical verbal or non-verbal conduct of sexual nature may consist not of a single act but of pattern of behaviour comprising many such acts.

Noting that in some cases, the psychological stigma of reporting the conduct of a co-worker might require a great deal of courage on the part of the victim and they may report such acts after a long period of time. The guidelines suggest that the compliance mechanism should ensure time-bound treatment of complaints, but they do not suggest that a report can only be made within a short period of time since the incident occurred. Often, the police refuse to lodge FIRs for sexual harassment cases, especially where the harassment occurred some time ago.

CHAPTER SEVEN

Consumer Protection Act, 1986

The Consumer Protection Act,1986 (COPRA) was an Act of the Parliament of India enacted to protect the interests of consumers in India. It was replaced by the Consumer Protection Act, 2019. It was made for the establishment of consumer councils and other authorities for the settlement of consumer's grievances and matters connected with it. The act was passed in Assembly in October 1986 and came into force on December 24, 1986. The statute on the right was made before this COPRA act.

Significance of the Act

This Act is regarded as the 'Magna Carta' in the field of consumer protection for checking unfair trade practices, 'defects in goods' and 'deficiencies in services' as far as India is concerned. It has led to the establishment of a widespread network of consumer forums and appellate courts all over India. It has significantly impacted how businesses approach consumers and have empowered consumers to a greater extent.

Consumer Protection Council

Consumer Protection Councils are established at the national, state and district level to increase consumer awareness.

Various Consumer Organisations

To increase the awareness of consumers, there are many consumer organisations and NGOs that have been established.

CONSUMER GUIDANCE SOCIETY OF INDIA (CGSI) was THE FIRST CONSUMER ORGANISATION ESTABLISHED IN INDIA IN 1966.

It was followed by many others such as

(1) Consumer Education And Research Centre (Gujarat)

(2) Bureau Of Indian Standards

(3) Federation Of Consumer Organisation In Tamil Nadu

(4) Mumbai Grahak Panchayat

(5) Consumer Voice (New Delhi)

(6) Legal Aid Society (Kolkata)

(7) Akhil Bhartiya Grahak Panchayat

(8) The Consumers Eye India.

(9)United India Consumer's Association.

Consumer Disputes Redressal Agencies

Main article: Consumer Court

- District Consumer Disputes Redressal Forum (DCDRF): Also known as the "District Forum" established by the State Government in each district of the State. The State Governments may establish more than one District

Forum in a district. It is a district-level court that deals with cases valuing up to ?2 million (US$27,000).

- State Consumer Disputes Redressal Commission (SCDRC): Also known as the "State Commission" established by the State Government in the State. It is a state-level court that takes up cases valuing less than ?10 million (US$130,000)
- National Consumer Disputes Redressal Commission (NCDRC): Established by the Central Government. It deals with matters of more than 10 million.

Objectives of the central council

The objectives of the Central Council is to promote and to protect the rights of the consumers such as:-

1. The right to be protected against the marketing of goods and services which are hazardous to life and property.
2. The right to be informed about the quality, quantity, potency, purity, standard and price of goods or services, as the case may be to protect the consumer against unfair trade practices;
3. The right to be assured, wherever possible, access to a variety of goods and services at competitive prices ;
4. The right to be heard and to be assured that consumer's interest will receive due consideration at appropriate forums;
5. The right to seek redressal against unfair trade practices or restrictive trade practices or unscrupulous exploitation of consumers
6. The right to consumer education.

Jurisdiction/Three Tier System of Council Courts

- **Jurisdiction of District Forum**

Subject to the other provisions of this Act, the District Forum shall have jurisdiction to entertain complaints where the value of the goods or services and the compensation, if any, claimed does not exceed rupees one crore.

A complaint shall be instituted in a District Forum within the local limits of whose jurisdiction:-

a) – the opposite party or each of the opposite parties, where there are more than one, at the time of the institution of the complaint, actually and voluntarily resides or carries on business or has a branch office or personally works for gain, or

b) – any of the opposite parties, where there are more than one, at the time of the institution of the complaint, actually and voluntarily resides, or carries on business or has a branch office, or personally works for gain, provided that in such case either the permission of the District Forum is given, or the opposite parties who do not reside, or carry on business or have a branch office, or personally work for gain, as the case may be, acquiesce in such institution; or

c) – the cause of action, wholly or in part, arises.

Consumer courts do not have jurisdiction over matters where services or goods were bought for a commercial purpose.

- **Jurisdiction of State Commission**

Subject to the other provisions of this Act, the State Commission shall have jurisdiction:-

a) to entertain

i) complaints where the value of the goods or services and compensation, if any, claimed exceeds rupees one crore but does not exceed rupees ten crore; and

ii) appeals against the orders of any District Forum within the State; and

b) to call for the records and pass appropriate orders in any consumer dispute.

- **Jurisdiction of National Commission**

(a) to entertain—

(i) complaints where the value of the goods or services and compensation, if any, claimed exceeds rupees ten crore; and

(ii) appeals against the orders of any State mayor; and

(b) to call for the records and pass appropriate orders in any consumer dispute which is pending before or has been decided by any State Commission. However, the Supreme Court of India has held that the jurisdiction of National Commission under Revision Jurisdiction is very limited and can only be exercised when State Commission exceeds its jurisdiction, fails to exercise its jurisdiction or there is material illegality in the order passed by State Commission.

CHAPTER EIGHT

Consumer Rights

The term **"consumer"** has been defined in **Section 2 (1) (d) of the Consumer Protection Act, 1986** as: **"any person who buys any goods for consideration or hires/avails any services for consideration".**

The Consumer Protection Act, 1986, as amended in August 2019, provides protection to the interests of the consumers and aims at resolving their disputes. One of the main question of law that is always raised at the time of deciding a consumer complaint is whether the complainant falls within the definition of consumer as enumerated under the Consumer Protection Act, 1986?

Consumer Rights

World Consumer Rights Day: Six consumer rights every Indian must know!

Every year on March 15 World Consumer Rights Day is celebrated. According to Consumers International website, 'the consumer movement marks March 15 with World Consumer Rights Day every year, as a means of raising global awareness about consumer rights and needs. However, Celebrating this day is a chance to demand that the rights of all consumers are protected and respected, and to protest against social injustices and market abuses which undermine those rights.' In India, the Consumer Protection Act, 1986, deals with the rights that ensure consumers in the country get goods and services worth their money. The act was passed in the assembly in October 1986 to protect the interests of consumers in India. Under the Consumer Protection Act, 1986, the government of India gives us six basic rights that every Indian must know.

1. **Right to Safety :**Right to Safety is referred to as 'right to be protected against the marketing of goods and services which are hazardous to life and property'. It is mainly applicable in healthcare, pharmaceuticals, and food processing sectors. The right is also applicable in sectors that have an indirect impact on health including automobiles, housing, domestic appliances, and travel.
2. **Right to Information :** The Consumer Protection Act, 1986, defines Right to Information as 'the right to be informed about the quality, quantity, potency, purity, standard and price of goods so as to protect the consumer against unfair trade practices'. For instance, the consumers need to make aware of the cost involved for availing a loan, or pharmaceuticals must disclose the potentials side effects of drugs.
3. **Right to Choose :** Referred to as 'the right to be assured, wherever possible, access to a variety of goods at competitive prices'. Did you know a consumer can even bargain on the MRP, as it is not fixed by the government and the actual selling price could be lower depending on the taxes?
4. **Right to be Heard :** The Act defines the 'Right to Heard' as, 'the right to be heard and to be assured that consumers' interests will receive due consideration at

appropriate forums'. The right ensures that consumers come forward without any fear, file the complaint and raise their voice against any products and services. There are websites that let consumers upload their grievances which are later verified and forwarded to the consumer courts for redressal.

5. **Right to Redressal :** The Right to Redressal means, 'the right to seek redressal against unfair trade practices or unscrupulous exploitation of consumers'. With the help of the Consumer Protection Act, consumer courts are incorporated for consumers to seek redressal against unfair trade practices or exploitation. These courts are set on three levels which includes District Consumer Disputes Redressal Forums at the district level, State Consumer Disputes Redressal Commissions at the state level and National Consumer Disputes Redressal Commissions at the national level.

9 Essential Remedies Available to Consumers under Indian Consumer Protections Act

a. **Removal of Defects:** If after proper testing the product proves to be defective, then the 'remove its defects' order can be passed by the authority concerned.
b. **Replacement of Goods:** Orders can be passed to replace the defective product by a new non-defective product of the same type.
c. **Refund of Price:** Orders can be passed to refund the price paid by the complainant for the product.
d. **Award of Compensation:** If because of the negligence of the seller a consumer suffers physical or any other loss,

then compensation for that loss can be demanded for.

e. **Removal of Deficiency in Service:** If there is any deficiency in delivery of service, then orders can be passed to remove that deficiency. For instance, if an insurance company makes unnecessary delay in giving final touch to the claim, then under this Act orders can be passed to immediately finalise the claim.
f. **Discontinuance of Unfair/Restrictive** Trade Practice: If a complaint is filed against unfair/restrictive trade practice, then under the Act that practice can be banned with immediate effect. For instance, if a gas company makes it compulsory for a consumer to buy gas stove with the gas connection, then this type of restrictive trade practice can be checked with immediate effect.
g. **Stopping the Sale of Hazardous Goods:** Products which can prove hazardous for life, their sale can be stopped.

(h) Withdrawal of Hazardous Goods from the Market: On seeing the serious adverse effects of hazardous goods on the consumers, such goods can be withdrawn from the market. The objective of doing so that such products should not be offered for sale.

(i) Payment of Adequate Cost: In the end, there is a provision in this Act that the trader should pay adequate cost to the victim concerned.

CHAPTER NINE

Fundamental rights of citizens

Fundamental Right is a charter of rights contained in the Constitution of India. Fundamental Rights assured all Indians to ensure that we live in peace and harmony as citizens of India. In this article, we look at the Fundamental Rights of Indian citizens as per the Indian Constitution.

- **Right to Equality** : The Right to equality ensures that every citizen is the same under the law. Hence, any person irrespective of age, gender, caste, creed, religion, language, and social status are considered equal. The Right to equality ensures that all persons are treated equally. The Right to equality discriminates on the grounds of religion, race, caste, gender or place of birth, and equality – illegal in India.

The following Articles in the Constitution ensure the Right to equality for all Indians:

Article 14: Equality before the law

Article 15: Prohibition of discrimination on grounds only of sex, religion, race, caste, or place of birth.

Article 16: Equality of opportunity in matters of public employment

Article 17: Abolition of untouchability

Article 18: Abolition of titles, Military, and academic distinctions are exempted.

- **Right to Freedom :** Indian Citizens enjoy six freedoms as per the Constitution. The Right to freedom ensures that Indian citizens can carry out their daily lives peacefully without undue restriction, harassment, or oversight by the Government.

Six fundamental freedom provided under Article 19 of the Constitution are:

1. Freedom of speech and expression
2. Freedom to assemble peacefully without arms
3. Freedom to form associations or unions or co-operative societies
4. Freedom to move freely throughout the territory of India
5. Freedom to reside and settle in any part of the territory of India
6. Freedom to practise any profession or to carry on any occupation, trade or business

In addition to Article 19 above, the following Articles of the Constitution ensure the Right to freedom for all Indian Citizens:

Article 20: Protection in respect of conviction for offences

Article 21: Protection of life and personal liberty

Article 22: Protection against arrest and detention in certain cases.

- **Right against Exploitation :** All Indian Citizens enjoy a right against being exploited or misused. The Right against exploitation provided under the Constitution protects children, the vulnerable and the poor from bonded labour, child labour, and human trafficking.

The following Articles in the Constitution ensure Right against exploitation for all Indians:

Article 23: Prohibition of traffic in human beings and forced labour

Article 24: Prohibition of employment of children (Employment for the Indian below the age of 14 years is not possible.)

- **Right to Freedom of Religion :** India is a secular country with people of different faiths living in harmony. Indian citizens can practice a religion of choice and perform rituals or activities as per their religious customs. According to the Constitution, all religions are equal before the State, and no religion has a preference over the other. Further, Indian Citizens are free to preach, practise, and propagate any religion of their choice.

The following Articles in the Constitution ensure the Right to freedom of religion:

Article 25: Freedom of conscience and free profession, practice and propagation of religion

Article 26: Freedom to manage religious affairs

Article 27: Freedom to pay tax for promotion of any particular religion – No person is compelled to pay any taxes for the promotion or maintenance of any particular religion or religious denomination

Article 28: Freedom as to attendance at religious instruction or religious worship in certain educational institutions.

- **Cultural and Educational Rights :** The Cultural and Education Rights in the Constitution protect the rights and customs of the minorities. Further, the Constitution provides for any community that has a language, and a script of its own has the Right to conserve and develop it.

The following Articles in the Constitution protect cultural and education rights:

Article 29: Protection of interests of minorities

Article 30: Right of minorities to establish and administer educational institutions.

- **Right to Constitutional Remedies :** Right to Constitution Remedies empowers Indian citizens to approach a court of law, in case of any denial of the fundamental rights. This Right gives also empowers Courts to preserve or safeguard the citizens' fundamental rights as laid out in the Constitution.

Article: 32: Remedies for enforcement of rights

- **Right to information (RTI) :** Right to information has been given the status of a fundamental right under Article 19(1) of the Constitution in 2005. Article 19 (1) under which every citizen has freedom of speech and expression and the right to know how the government works, what roles it plays, what its functions are, and so on.

- **Right to privacy** : The right to privacy is protected as an intrinsic part of the right to life and personal liberty under Article 21 and as a part of the freedoms guaranteed by Part III of the Constitution. It protects the inner sphere of the individual from interference from both State and non-State actors and allows individuals to make autonomous life choices. On 24 August 2017, the Supreme Court of India[74][75][76][77] ruled that:

"Right to Privacy is an integral part of Right to Life and Personal Liberty guaranteed in Article 21 of the Constitution,"

enforcement of the Fundamental Rights

For the enforcement of the Fundamental Rights of an aggrieved citizen, the right to remedies is conferred under Article 32. Therefore, the right to get Fundamental Rights protected is in itself a fundamental right. This makes the Fundamental Rights real. The Supreme Court has made Article 32 a basic feature of the Constitution i.e. these rights cannot be taken away even by way of an amendment to the Constitution.

An aggrieved party, in case of violation of the Fundamental Rights, has the option of moving either the high court or the Supreme Court directly. However, the ruling of the Supreme Court states that wherever relief through the high court is available under Article 226, the aggrieved party should first move the high court.

The Supreme Court and the high court both can issue writs in case of the violation of fundamental rights of an aggrieved party. These writs include habeas corpus, certiorari, prohibition, quo-warranto, and mandamus. However, the writ jurisdiction of the Supreme Court differs from that of the high court in three respects. The writ jurisdiction (power to issue writs) of the Supreme Court is narrower than that of the high court. Whereas the territorial jurisdiction of the Supreme Court is wider than that of the high court.

Rights in relation to police

Rights to a person before he/she deals with Police

- **Section 29** of the Indian Police Act, 1861 states that if a person is at the end of the misconduct due to a police officer's omission of duty, the officer may be punished with up to 3 months' imprisonment and up to 3 months' salary penalty.
- **Police Complaint Authority (PCA)** was formed in 2006 for managing police complaints and improving the police system's framework and way of operating. If there is a case of 'serious wrongdoing' the police officer may be found responsible. Anybody who has experienced police brutality will lodge a lawsuit with PCA.
- The courts have explicitly given rules specifying that, during the inquiry, a police officer can not intimidate people and must write down minutes of the inquiry in the station log or the daily journal.
- Only if the information does not reveal a cognizable offence and to the extent of finding the recognizability of a crime alone can preliminary inquiry be conducted. If a cognizable offence is revealed in the documents,

the police must file an FIR, so they can not obstruct the operation under the pretext of a preliminary investigation.

- Where a police officer fails to file an FIR, the informant can send the details to the Police Superintendent in writing. The witness or the perpetrator can even file with the Magistrate his / her case.
- If a person is summoned on the basis of being mentioned in a petition or listed as a witness, the police officer shall request a formal subpoena under Section 160 of the Code of Criminal Practice, 1973, stating the date and time for attendance.
- It's also suggested that an advocate can join you if you go to the police department to lodge a lawsuit against a police officer.
- During the event of police detention, there are two records you need to know about; search memo, and detention memo. An inspection memo is important because it states how you look like before being locked up and if you have any injuries before being locked up or not, so you won't get injured during the investigation. Memo of Detention has clear details about the incident, including witness names, and there are no lies heard by the police perspective.

Rights of an arrested person before he/she deals with Police

- **Section 46** of the CrPC contemplates forms of detention, i.e. surrender to imprisonment, physical handling of the body, or confining it. The arrest is a curtailment of human rights. When subjected to jail, by gestures, or by actions, detention will be affected by physical communication. When force is required, it should not be more than is justly necessary because this provision does not grant the power to inflict death to a person who is not charged with a crime punishable by death or life imprisonment. Where a woman is to be detained, the police officer shall not contact the woman's body for making an arrest unless the police officer is a woman, who will be believed to be detained on her submission to custody on oral intimation.

- **Section 50(1)** of the CrPC provides that "any police officer or other person arresting any person without a warrant shall forthwith communicate to him full details of the offence for which he is being arrested or other reasons for such arrest." Apart from the provisions of the CrPC, Article 22(1) of the Constitution of India provides that "No person arrested shall be held in custody without, as soon as possible, being told of the reasons for such detention, nor shall he be refused the right to consult and defend a legal practitioner of his choosing." Centred on Supreme Court decisions in Joginder Kumar v. The State of UP, (1994) 4 SCC 260 and D.K. Basu v. West Bengal State, (1997) 1 SCC 416 Substantial amendments were enacted in Section 50-A of the CrPC in 2006 making it compulsory for the police officer to make an arrest to inform the arrested person's friend, relative or any nominee about his arrest, to inform the arrested person of his rights and to enter the register maintained by the police. In this way, the judge is therefore under a duty to inform himself of police action.

- Under Section 41 of the CrPC, broad powers are bestowed on police to apprehend, especially in committed crimes, without having to go to the Magistrate and seek an apprehend warrant. No lawful arrest may occur if there is no evidence or fair belief that the person has been engaged in a cognizable crime or commits the offence (s) listed in Section 41. The responsibility is on the police officer to convince the court who has the fairground of doubt in which the detention is questioned. With the exception of the above, Section 45 of the CrPC provides that members of the Armed Forces may not be arrested for anything done in the performance of official duties, except with the central government's consent.
- Section 54 of the CrPC allows for compulsory medical examination by a medical officer in the service of federal or state government, or by a licensed medical practitioner, in the case of any medical officer being unavailable. Only female police officers or licensed medical professionals may treat female arrestees. However, Sections 53 & 53A of the CrPC specify that if there are fairgrounds for assuming that an inspection of the accused person on charges of rape or other crime would include evidence for the conduct of any crime, it is lawful to inspect the blood, blood traces, sperm, hair samples, fingernail cuts using modern and experimental techniques including DNA and so on.
- Section 49 of the CrPC states that there should be no more restriction than is justly appropriate to deter escape, i.e. fair force may, if required, be used for the purpose; but an arrest must take place before a person is held under some sort of constraint. It is unconstitutional to seize or prosecute without detention.

- Section 50(2) of the CrPC provides that any person arrested without a warrant shall be informed immediately of the reasons for his arrest and, where the arrest is made in a bailable case, the person shall be informed of his right to be released on bail. Section 50 is compulsory and fulfils the requirement given for in Article 22(1) of the Indian Constitution.
- CrPC, Section 51 requires a police officer to conduct a personal search of the people detained. Concerning the provisions of this clause, reference can be made to Article 20(3) of the Indian Constitution, which is a protection against self-incriminating testimonial coercion for the convicted. While an accused can not be compelled to show any evidence against him, by obtaining a search warrant, he can be taken by statute from the possession of the property of the accused.
- Whereas a person has the freedom to meet and to be represented by a lawyer of his choosing following the arrest; the arrester has the right to free legal assistance. A society under the rule of law always has an obligation, aside from maintaining equal punishment, to provide for the protection of the criminal if he is too weak to do so. Free legal assistance to people of minimal means is a privilege that the modern State, particularly a welfare state, owes to its residents.

It is important to follow scrupulously the civil and legal requirements to present an accused person before a Judicial Magistrate within 24 hours of the arrest (Khatri v. State of Bihar, AIR 1983 SC 378). Section 57 applies exclusively to the issue of the incarceration period. The intention is to bring the accused with the least delay to a competent magistrate to try or commit. The right to be released from police custody by being taken before a Magistrate is essential to avoid apprehension and imprisonment, with a view to obtaining evidence or as a way of forcing individuals to give information

Right to seek bail implicit in Constitution: Supreme Court

The Supreme Court has held that the right to apply for bail is an "individual right" implicit in the Constitution.

"The right of an accused, an undertrial prisoner or a convicted person awaiting appeal court's verdict to seek bail on suspension of sentence is recognised in Sections 439, 438 and 389 of the Code of Criminal Procedure," a judgment by a Bench of Justices L. Nageswara Rao and Aniruddha Bose said.

The court was hearing a case in which a Single Judge of the Rajasthan High Court had in March passed an order to not to list bails, appeals, applications for suspension of sentence in appeals and revisions in the category of extreme urgent matters.

"If there is a blanket ban on listing of these applications, even for offences with lesser degree of punishment, that would effectively block access for seekers of liberty to apply for bail and in substance suspend the fundamental rights of individuals in or apprehending detention. Such an order also has the effect of temporarily eclipsing statutory provisions," Justice Bose, who authored the judgment, observed.

The court noted that the same judge had in May directed the police authorities not to make arrest of persons in cases where the accused is charged under an offence carrying maximum sentence of three years and the offence is triable by a First Class Magistrate.

In this order also, direction had been given to the High Court administration not to list bail applications in offences where maximum sentence extends upto three years and the offence which is triable by a First Class Magistrate.

When these orders were passed, the Covid-19 pandemic was raging across this country.

The apex court noted that both directions, in March and May, "had the potential for breaching the constitutional and legal rights of individuals who could be or are arraigned in criminal action and also put fetters on power of investigating agencies."

searches and seizures

The Constitution, through the Fourth Amendment, protects people from unreasonable searches and seizures by the government. The Fourth Amendment, however, is not a guarantee against all searches and seizures, but only those that are deemed unreasonable under the law.

Whether a particular type of search is considered reasonable in the eyes of the law, is determined by balancing two important interests. On one side of the scale is the intrusion on an individual's Fourth Amendment rights. On the other side of the scale are legitimate government interests, such as public safety.

The extent to which an individual is protected by the Fourth Amendment depends, in part, on the location of the search or seizure. Minnesota v. Carter, 525 U.S. 83 (1998).

Home

Searches and seizures inside a home without a warrant are presumptively unreasonable.

Payton v. New York, 445 U.S. 573 (1980).

However, there are some exceptions. A warrantless search may be lawful:

If an officer is given consent to search; Davis v. United States, 328 U.S. 582 (1946)

If the search is incident to a lawful arrest; United States v. Robinson, 414 U.S. 218 (1973)

If there is probable cause to search and exigent circumstances; Payton v. New York, 445 U.S. 573 (1980)

If the items are in plain view; Maryland v. Macon, 472 U.S. 463 (1985)

A Person

When an officer observes unusual conduct which leads him reasonably to conclude that criminal activity may be afoot, the officer may briefly stop the suspicious person and make reasonable inquiries aimed at confirming or dispelling the officer's suspicions.

Terry v. Ohio, 392 U.S. 1 (1968)

Minnesota v. Dickerson, 508 U.S. 366 (1993)

Schools

School officials need not obtain a warrant before searching a student who is under their authority; rather, a search of a student need only be reasonable under all the circumstances.

New Jersey v. TLO, 469 U.S. 325 (1985)

Cars

Where there is probable cause to believe that a vehicle contains evidence of a criminal activity, an officer may lawfully search any area of the vehicle in which the evidence might be found.

Arizona v. Gant, 129 S. Ct. 1710 (2009),

An officer may conduct a traffic stop if he has reasonable suspicion that a traffic violation has occurred or that criminal activity is afoot.

Berekmer v. McCarty, 468 U.S. 420 (1984),

United States v. Arvizu, 534 U.S. 266 (2002).

An officer may conduct a pat-down of the driver and passengers during a lawful traffic stop; the police need not believe that any occupant of the vehicle is involved in a criminal activity.

Arizona v. Johnson, 555 U.S. 323 (2009).

The use of a narcotics detection dog to walk around the exterior of a car subject to a valid traffic stop does not require reasonable, explainable suspicion.

Illinois v. Cabales, 543 U.S. 405 (2005).

Special law enforcement concerns will sometimes justify highway stops without any individualized suspicion.

Illinois v. Lidster, 540 U.S. 419 (2004).

An officer at an international border may conduct routine stops and searches.

United States v. Montoya de Hernandez, 473 U.S. 531 (1985).

A state may use highway sobriety checkpoints for the purpose of combating drunk driving.

Michigan Dept. of State Police v. Sitz, 496 U.S. 444 (1990).

A state may set up highway checkpoints where the stops are brief and seek voluntary cooperation in the investigation of a recent crime that has occurred on that highway.

Illinois v. Lidster, 540 U.S. 419 (2004).

However, a state may not use a highway checkpoint program whose primary purpose is the discovery and interdiction of illegal narcotics.

City of Indianapolis v. Edmond, 531 U.S. 32 (2000).

Rights of a woman against police

- **Right to free aid** : When a woman goes to the police station without being accompanied by a lawyer she is either quoted wrong, ignored or humiliated for her statements. She should be aware of the fact that she has a right to get the legal aid and that she should demand for it. "According to a Delhi High Court ruling, whenever a rape is reported, the senior house officer has to bring this to the notice of the Delhi Legal Services Authority. The legal body then arranges for a lawyer for the victim," says Saumya Bhaumik, a women rights lawyer.
- **Right to privacy** : A woman who has been raped has a right to record her statement in private, in front of the magistrate without being overheard by anyone else. She also has a freedom to record her statement with a lady constable or a police officer in personal. Under section 164 of the Criminal Procedure Code, the cops will have to give the privacy to the victim without stressing her in front of masses.
- **Right to untimely registration** : There are many reasons as to why a woman would postpone going to the police to lodge a complaint. She considers her reputation, dignity of the family and threats from the culprit to take her life away. Police in any way cannot say no to register her complaint, no matter if it's too late to register. The self-respect of women comes before anything else. She cannot be denied of anything.
- **Right to virtual complaints** : According to the guidelines issued by the Delhi Police, a woman has the privilege of lodging a complaint via email or registered

post. If, for some reason, a woman can't go to the police station, she can send a written complaint through an email or registered post addressed to a senior police officer of the level of Deputy Commissioner or Commissioner of Police. The officer then directs the SHO of the police station, of the area where the incident occurred, to conduct proper verification of the complainant and lodge an FIR. The police can then come over to the residence of the victim to take her statement.

- **Right to Zero FIR :** A rape victim can register her police complaint from any police station under the Zero FIR ruling by Supreme Court. "Sometimes, the police station under which the incident occurs refuses to register the victim's complaint in order to keep clear of responsibility, and tries sending the victim to another police station. In such cases, she has the right to lodge an FIR at any police station in the city under the Zero FIR ruling. The senior officer will then direct the SHO of the concerned police station to lodge the FIR," says Abeed. This is a Supreme Court ruling that not many women are aware of, so don't let the SHO of a police station send you away saying it "doesn't come under his area".
- **Right to no arrest :** According to a Supreme Court ruling, a woman cannot be arrested after sunset and before sunrise. There are many cases of women being harassed by the police at wee hours, but all this can be avoided if you exercise the right of being present in the police station only during daytime. "Even if there is a woman constable accompanying the officers, the police can't arrest a woman at night. In case the woman has committed a serious crime, the police requires to get it in writing from the magistrate explaining why the arrest

is necessary during the night," says Bhaumik.

- **Right to not being called to the police station :** Women cannot be called to the police station for interrogation under Section 160 of the Criminal Procedure Code. This law provides Indian women the right of not being physically present at the police station for interrogation. "The police can interrogate a woman at her residence in the presence of a woman constable and family members or friends," says Abeed. So, the next time you're called to the police station for queries or interrogation when you have faced any kind of harassment, quote this guideline of the Supreme Court to exercise your right and remind the cops about it.
- **Right to confidentiality** : Under no circumstances can the identity of a rape victim be revealed. Neither the police nor media can make known the name of the victim in public. Section 228-A of the Indian Penal Code makes the disclosure of a victim's identity a punishable offense. Printing or publishing the name or any matter which may make known the identity of a woman against whom an offense has been committed is punishable. This is done to prevent social victimization or ostracism of the victim of a sexual offense. Even while a judgment is in progress at the high court or a lower court, the name of the victim is not indicated, she is only described as 'victim' in the judgment.
- **Right towards crime and not a medical condition** : A case of rape can't be dismissed even if the doctor says that rape has not taken place. A victim of rape needs to be medically examined as per Section 164 A of the Criminal Procedure Code, and only the report can act as proof. "A woman has the right to have a copy of the medical report from the doctor. Rape is crime and

not a medical condition. It is a legal term and not a diagnosis to be made by the medical officer treating the victim. The only statement that can be made by the medical officer is that there is evidence of recent sexual activity. Whether the rape has occurred or not is a legal conclusion and the doctor can't decide on this," explains Bhaumik.

- **Right to no sexual harassment :** It is the duty of every employer to create a Sexual Harassment Complaints Committee within the organization for complaints. According to a guideline issued by the Supreme Court, it is mandatory for all firms, public and private, to set up these committees to resolve matters of sexual harassment. It is also necessary that the committee be headed by a woman and comprise of 50% women, as members. Also, one of the members should be from a women's welfare group.

CHAPTER TEN

Right to Information

RTI stands for Right to Information. Right to Information Act 2005 mandates timely response to citizen requests for government information. Right to Information empowers every citizen to seek any information from the Government, inspect any Government documents and seek certified photocopies thereof. Right to Information also empowers citizens to official inspect any Government work or to take the sample of material used in any work.

Right to Information is a part of fundamental rights under Article 19(1) of the Constitution. Article 19 (1) says that every citizen has freedom of speech and expression.

Even though RTI is a fundamental right, still we need RTI Act to give us this right. This is because if you went to any Government Department and told the officer there, "RTI is my fundamental right and that I am the master of this country. Therefore, please show me all your files", he would not do that. In all probability, he would throw you out of his room. Therefore, we need a machinery or a process through which we can exercise this fundamental right. Right to Information Act 2005, which became effective on 13th October 2005, provides that machinery. Therefore, Right to Information Act does not give us any new right. It simply lays down the process on how to apply for information, where to apply, how much fees etc.

Who can ask for information under Right to Information?

Any citizen can ask for information under these laws.The Act extends to the whole of India except the State of Jammu and Kashmir. OCI's (Overseas Citizens of India) and PIO's (Persons of Indian Origin) card holders can also ask for information under the RTI Act.

For citizens, OCI's and PIO's who are staying out of India, the RTI Application can be filed with the PIO of the local Indian Embassy/Consulate/High Commission and they will inform you regarding the amount of application fee in local currency as well as the mode of payment.

Grounds for Rejection under RTI

here are only three possible grounds on which information can be denied:

- The organisation is not a Public authority - eg. a Cooperative Society, or a Private corporate or Institution, not substantially financed or controlled by the Government.
- What is asked for 'not information' as defined under the Act: Information has to exist. Interpretations of law or decisions which do not exist, or reasons for decisions which do not exist will not be covered under the definition of 'information'
- The information asked for falls in the exemptions of Section 8(1) or under Section 9 applies. Section 9 bars giving information which would violate private party

copyright.

- Providing extracts from the records is required to be done as per Section 2(j)(ii) unless it would require too much time. If giving the information would require too much of the resource of the Public authority, it cannot refuse to give the information.
- If the form in which the applicant has asked for information would require too much time of the Public authority, it may offer it in another format. A common practice adopted by PIOs when the information gathering or collating in a particular format would require excessive time is to offer inspection of files to the applicant.

remedies for not furnishing the information under RTI

In such a case, you are required to file your appeal in physical mode to the concerned public authority. 2) Another case can be if your RTI application has not been replied to by CPIO and 30 days period has not lapsed. In such a case, you may file first appeal only after completion of stipulated time period of 30 days

CHAPTER ELEVEN

Lokayukt – object, function, power and duties

The Lokayukta is an anti-corruption authority constituted at the state level. It investigates allegations of corruption and mal-administration against public servants and is tasked with speedy redressal of public grievances.

The origin of the Lokayukta can be traced to the Ombudsmen in Scandinavian countries. The Administrative Reforms Commission, (1966-70), had recommended the creation of the Lokpal at the Centre and Lokayukta in the states. The Centre is yet to get a Lokpal.

The Lokayukta is created as a statutory authority with a fixed tenure to enable it to discharge its functions independently and impartially. The person appointed is usually a former High Court Chief Justice or former Supreme Court judge.

Members of the public can directly approach the Lokayukta with complaints of corruption, nepotism or any other form of mal-administration against any government official.

Or

The Lokpal and Lokayukta Act 2013,makes it compulsory for each state to appoint Lokayukta similar to Lokpal at central level for investigation into complaints of corruption against government officers in public offices. As per the Act the institution should have both Judicial and Non-Judicial members. Lokayukta investigates cases of corruption committed at state level, and once proved recommends action. It is a great check on corruption, brings about transparency in the system, makes administrative machinery citizen friendly. His functions largely depend upon jurisdiction vested in him and facilities provided for taking cognizance of citizens' grievances promptly, dexterously and expeditiously through simple, informal mechanism devoid of technicalities.

Institution of Lokpal has not as yet been created at the centre, although efforts have been made since 1959. Meanwhile, Lokayuktas/Lokpal have been established by many states through state legislations. They provide for inquiry/investigation into complaints of corruption against public servants. He protects Citizens' Right against mal-administration, corruption, delay, inefficiency, non-transparency, abuse of position, improper conduct etc. To keep the powers of Lokayukta neutral and non-biased provision for fixed tenure is made.[5] The procedure to be followed is informal and inexpensive; technicalities do not come in way. Complaint is supported by affidavit, making out case for inquiry. He is representative of Legislature, powerful friend of citizens to act against officials action, inaction or corruption. But not anti-administration, rather helps in humanizing relations between the public and the administration, a step forward in establishing an 'Open Government' securing respect for the rule of law, an educator aiming at propagating the prevention of corruption, inefficiency and mal-administration in governance. He is, therefore, a check on corruption.

Constitutional Amendment for Effectiveness

An amendment to the Constitution has been proposed to implement the Lokayukta uniformly across Indian states. The proposed changes will make the institution of Lokayukta uniform across the country as a three-member body, headed by a retired Supreme Court judge or high court chief justice and comprising the state vigilance commissioner and a jurist or an eminent administrator as other members

CHAPTER TWELVE

Children Education ACT 2009

1. Every child between the ages of 6 to 14 years has the right to free and compulsory education. This is stated as per the 86th Constitution Amendment Act via Article 21A. The Right to Education Act seeks to give effect to this amendment
2. The government schools shall provide free education to all the children and the schools will be managed by School Management Committees (SMC). Private schools shall admit at least 25% of the children in their schools without any fee.
3. The National Commission for Elementary Education shall be constituted to monitor all aspects of elementary education including quality.

Main Features of Right to Education (RTE) Act, 2009

- Free and compulsory education to all children of India in the 6 to 14 age group.
- No child shall be held back, expelled or required to pass a board examination until the completion of elementary education.
- If a child above 6 years of age has not been admitted in any school or could not complete his or her elementary education, then he or she shall be admitted in a class appropriate to his or her age. However, if a case may be where a child is directly admitted in the class appropriate to his or her age, then, in order to be at par with others, he or she shall have a right to receive special training within such time limits as may be prescribed. Provided further that a child so admitted to elementary education shall be entitled to free education till the completion of elementary education even after 14 years.
- Proof of age for admission: For the purpose of admission to elementary education, the age of a child shall be determined on the basis of the birth certificate issued in accordance with the Provisions of Birth. Deaths and Marriages Registration Act 1856, or on the basis of such other document as may be prescribed.No child shall be denied admission in a school for lack of age proof
- A child who completes elementary education shall be awarded a certificate.
- Call need to be taken for a fixed student–teacher ratio.
- Twenty-five per cent reservation for economically disadvantaged communities in admission to Class I in all private schools is to be done.
- Improvement in the quality of education is important.
- School teachers will need adequate professional degree within five years or else will lose job.

- School infrastructure (where there is a problem) need to be improved in every 3 years, else recognition will be cancelled.
- Financial burden will be shared between the state and the central government.

Scope of RTE Act

1. Compulsory and free education for all

It is obligatory for the Government to provide free and compulsory elementary education to each and every child, in a neighbourhood school within 1 km, up to class 8 in India. No child is liable to pay fees or any other charges that may prevent him or her from pursuing and completing elementary education. Free education also includes the provisions of textbooks, uniforms, stationery items and special educational material for children with disabilities in order to reduce the burden of school expenses.

2. The benchmark mandate

The Right to Education Act lays down norms and standards relating to Pupil-Teacher-Ratios (number of children per teacher), classrooms, separate toilets for girls and boys, drinking water facility, number of school-working days, working hours of teachers, etc. Each and every elementary school (Primary school + Middle School) in India has to comply with this set of norms to maintain a minimum standard set by the Right to Education Act.

3. Special provisions for special cases

The Right to Education Act mandates that an out of school child should be admitted to an age-appropriate class and provided with special training to enable the child to come up to age-appropriate learning level.

4. Quantity and quality of teachers

The Right to Education Act provides for rational deployment of teachers by ensuring that the specified Pupil-Teacher-Ratio is maintained in every school with no urban-rural imbalance whatsoever. It also mandates appointing appropriately trained teachers i.e. teachers with the requisite entry and academic qualifications.

5. Zero tolerance against discrimination and harassment

The Right to Education Act 2009 prohibits all kinds of physical punishment and mental harassment, discrimination based on gender, caste, class and religion, screening procedures for admission of children capitation fee, private tuition centres, and functioning of unrecognised schools.

The Right to Education (RTE) Forum's Stocktaking Report 2014 suggested that across the country, less than 10 per cent of schools comply with all of the Right to Education Act norms and standards. While the enactment of the Right to Education Act 2009 triggered significant improvements, concerns regarding the privatisation of education remain. Educational inequalities have held a strong ground in India for many years. While the Right to Education Act offers the first step towards an inclusive education system in India, effective implementation of the same still remains to be a challenge.

6. Ensuring all-round development of children

The Right to Education Act 2009 provides for the development of a curriculum, which would ensure the all-around development of every child. Build a child's knowledge, human potential and talent.

7. Improving learning outcomes to minimise detention

The Right to Education Act mandates that no child can be held back or expelled from school till Class 8. To improve the performances of children in schools, the Right to Education Act introduced the Continuous Comprehensive Evaluation (CCE) system in 2009 to ensure grade-appropriate learning outcomes in schools. Another reason why this system was initiated was to evaluate every aspect of the child during their time in school so that gaps could be identified and worked on well in time.

8. Monitoring compliance of RTE norms

School Management Committees (SMCs) play a crucial role in strengthening participatory democracy and governance in elementary education. All schools covered under the Right to Education Act 2009 are obligated to constitute a School Management Committee comprising of a headteacher, local elected representative, parents, community members etc. The committees have been empowered to monitor the functioning of schools and to prepare a school development plan.

9. Right to Education Act is justiciable

The Right to Education Act is justiciable and is backed by a Grievance Redressal (GR) mechanism that allows people to take action against non-compliance of provisions of the Right to Education Act 2009.

To ensure all schools follow this mandate, Oxfam India in collaboration with JOSH filed a complaint at the Central Information Commission (CIC) in 2011 evoking Section 4 of the Right to Information Act (RTI Act) 2005. Section 4 of the RTI Act is a proactive disclosure section mandating all public authorities to share information with citizens about their functioning. Since schools are public authorities, compliance to Section 4 was demanded.

10. Creating inclusive spaces for all

The Right to Education Act 2009 mandates for all private schools to reserve 25 per cent of their seats for children belonging to socially disadvantaged and economically weaker sections. This provision of the Act is aimed at boosting social inclusion to provide for a more just and equal nation.

CHAPTER THIRTEEN

Property Rights

Property Rights of Women in India

Hindu Law

Daughters

- Daughters have equal right of inheritance as sons to their father's property.
- Daughters also have a share in the mother's property.
- The Hindu Succession (Amendment) Act, 2005 (39 of 2005) came into force from 9th September, 2005. the Amendment Act removes gender discriminatory provisions in the Hindu Succession Act, 1956 and gives the following rights to daughters

The daughter of a coparcener shall by birth become a coparcener in her own right in the same manner as the son;

The daughter has the same rights in the coparcenary property as she would have had if she had been a son;

The daughter shall be subject to the same liability in the said coparcenary property as that of a son;

The daughter is allotted the same share as is allotted to a son;

- A married daughter has no right to shelter in her parents' house, nor maintenance, charge for her being passed on to her husband. However, a married daughter has a right of residence if she is deserted, divorced or widowed.
- A woman has full rights over any property that she has earned or that has been gifted or willed to her, provided she has attained majority. She is free to dispose of these by sale, gift or will as she deems fit.

Wives

- A married woman has exclusive right over her individual property. Unless she gifts it in part or wholly to anyone. She is the sole owner and manager of her assets whether earned, inherited or gifted to her.
- Entitled to maintenance, support and shelter from her husband, or if her husband belongs to a joint family, then from the family.
- Upon partition of a joint family estate, between her husband and his sons, she is entitled to a share equal to as any other person. Similarly, upon the death of her husband, she is entitled to an equal share of his portion, together with her children and his mother.

Mothers

- She is entitled to maintenance from children who are not dependents. She is also a Class I heir.
- A widowed mother has a right to take a share equal to the share of a son if a partition of joint family estate takes place among the sons.
- All property owned by her may be disposed by sale, will or gift as she chooses.
- In case she dies intestate, her children inherit equally, regardless of their sex.

Maintenance

Section 125 of Criminal procedure code prescribes for maintenance of wives, children and parents.

If any person having sufficient means neglects or refuses to maintain-

- His wife, who is unable to maintain herself, or
- His legitimate or illegitimate minor child,
- His father or mother, unable to maintain himself or herself

Court in such cases may order such person to make a monthly allowance for maintenance to the wife, child or parents

- Order issued by a Magistrate of the first class
- Magistrate can also during the pendency of the proceeding order monthly allowance for the interim

maintenance

- Application for the monthly allowance for the interim maintenance and expenses of proceeding shall, as far as possible, be disposed of with in sixty days from the date of the service of notice of the application
- "Wife" includes a woman who has been divorced by, or has obtained a divorce from, her husband and has not remarried.

CHAPTER FOURTEEN

Human rights

Human rights are simply basic rights that every human is entitled to regardless of their nationality, age, ethnic origin, gender, religion or language. The Universal Declaration of Human Rights (UDHR) was adopted by the United Nations General Assembly in Paris on 10 December 1948

INTERNATIONAL HUMAN RIGHTS LAW

The Universal Declaration of Human Rights is an ideal standard held in common by nations around the world, but it bears no force of law. Thus, from 1948 to 1966, the UN Human Rights Commission's main task was to create a body of international human rights law based on the Declaration, and to establish the mechanisms needed to enforce its implementation and use.

The Human Rights Commission produced two major documents: the International Covenant on Civil and Political Rights (ICCPR) and the International Covenant on Economic, Social and Cultural Rights (ICESCR). Both became international law in 1976. Together with the Universal Declaration of Human Rights, these two covenants comprise what is known as the "International Bill of Human Rights."

The ICCPR focuses on issues such as the right to life, freedom of speech, religion and voting. The ICESCR focuses on food, education, health and shelter. Both covenants proclaim these rights for all people and forbid discrimination.

Furthermore, Article 26 of the ICCPR established a Human Rights Committee of the United Nations. Composed of eighteen human rights experts, the Committee is responsible for ensuring that each signatory to the ICCPR complies with its terms. The Committee examines reports submitted by countries every five years (to ensure they are in compliance with the ICCPR), and issues findings based on a country's performance.

Many countries that ratified the ICCPR also agreed that the Human Rights Committee may investigate allegations by individuals and organizations that the State has violated their rights. Before appealing to the Committee, the complainant must exhaust all legal recourse in the courts of that country. After investigation, the Committee publishes the results. These findings have great force. If the Committee upholds the allegations, the State must take measures to remedy the abuse.

CHAPTER FIFTEEN

Right to maintenance under Hindu law

Introduction

"Maintenance" is an amount payable by the husband to his wife who is unable to maintain herself either during the subsistence of marriage or upon separation or divorce. Various laws governing maintenance are as follows:

for Hindus – Hindu Marriage Act, 1955; Hindu Adoption and Maintenance Act, 1956

for Muslims – Muslim Women (Protection of Rights on Divorce) Act, 1986

for Parsis – Parsi Marriage and Divorce Act, 1936

for Christians – Divorce Act, 1869

secular laws – Criminal Procedure Code, 1973; Special Marriage Act,1954

Temporary Maintenance (pendente lite)

Temporary maintenance is granted by the court during the pendency of proceeding for divorce or separation to meet the immediate needs of the petitioner.

Under Section 24 of Hindu Marriage Act, 1955 either of the spouses, husband or wife can be granted relief if the court is satisfied that the applicant has no independent income sufficient for his or her support and necessary expenses of the proceedings pending under the Act.

Interim maintenance may also be claimed **under Section 125 CrPC** by the wife during the pendency of proceeding for regarding monthly allowance for **maintenance under Section 125(1) CrPC.**

Furthermore, **Section 36 of Special Marriage Act, 1954** also makes provision for the wife to seek expenses from the husband if it appears to the district court that she does not have independent income sufficient for her support and necessary expenses of proceedings under Chapters V or VI of that Act.

Still further, under Parsi Marriage and Divorce Act, 1936 either Parsi wife or husband is entitled to claim expenses where the proceeding is pending under the Act. **Section 39** of the Act which is substantially the same as **Section 36** of the Special Marriage Act makes a provision in this behalf.

Also, under **Section 36 of Divorce Act, 1869** which applies to persons professing Christain religion, a wife is entitled to expenses of proceeding under the Act and maintenance while the suit is pending.

All these provisions specify that the application for interim maintenance has to be disposed of within sixty days of service of notice on the respondent.

Criminal Procedure Code, 1973, Section 125 –

This section provides for maintenance not only to the wife but also to child and parents. Court may order a husband who has sufficient means but neglects or refuses to maintain his wife who is unable to maintain herself to provide monthly maintenance to her. However, wife shall not be entitled to receive maintenance if she is living in adultery, or refuses to live with husband without any sufficient reasons, or living separately with mutual consent.

Permanent Maintenance

It is the maintenance granted permanently after the disposal of the proceeding for divorce or separation.

Hindu Marriage Act, 1955, Section 25 – Applicant, either wife or husband is entitled to receive from the spouse for his/her maintenance and support a gross sum or monthly or periodical sum for a term not exceeding the applicant's lifetime or until he/she remarries or remains chaste.

Hindu Adoption and Maintenance Act, 1956, Section 18 – Hindu wife is entitled to be maintained by her husband during her lifetime. Wife also has a right to separate residence and maintenance if any of the condition in Section 18(2) [desertion, cruelty, leprosy, any other wife/ concubine living in the same house, conversion of religion or any other reasonable cause] is fulfilled until she remains chaste or does not convert to other religion. It may also be noted that Section 19 of this Act makes a provision for a widowed wife to be maintained by her father-in-law.

Criminal Procedure Code, 1973, Section 125 – This section provides for maintenance not only to the wife but also to child and parents. Court may order a husband who has sufficient means but neglects or refuses to maintain his wife who is unable to maintain herself to provide monthly maintenance to her. However, wife shall not be entitled to receive maintenance if she is living in adultery, or refuses to live with husband without any sufficient reasons, or living separately with mutual consent.

Special Marriage Act, 1954, Section 37 – This section is also similar to Section 40 of the Parsi Marriage and Divorce Act. The difference being that under this section maintenance may be claimed only by a wife against the husband from a court exercising jurisdiction under Chapters V or VI of the Act. An order made under this section may be modified or rescinded by the district court at the instance of the husband if it is shown that the wife has remarried or is not leading a chaste life.

Divorce Act, 1869, Section 37 – This section empowers the district court to order the husband to secure a reasonable gross sum to the wife or annual sum not exceeding her lifetime when a decree of dissolution or decree or judicial separation is obtained by the wife. While passing such order, the court may have regard to fortune of the wife, ability of the husband and conduct of the parties. The court may also order the husband to pay such monthly or weekly sum to the wife for her maintenance as the court may think reasonable. If subsequently, the husband becomes unable to make such payments, the court may discharge or modify such order.

CHAPTER SIXTEEN

Object and scope of vehicle claim tribunal

During the British regime, Indian Motor Vehicle Act of 1914 was ratified with an objective to regulate enforcement and to ensure the registration and licensing of vehicles and motorists to maintain road safety. This was replaced by 1939 Act which consolidated and amended the law relating to motor vehicles according to the development in road transport technology, pattern of passenger and freight movements and particularly the improved techniques in the motor vehicles management, this was later further substituted by MV Act, 1988. The 1988 Act was a significant law which established a new court named Motor Accidents Claims Tribunals which replaced civil courts in order to provide cheaper and speedier relief to the victims of accident of motor vehicles.

Earlier, the suit claiming compensation needed to be filed in civil court along with an ad- valorem court fee. Since, the civil courts had a backlog of cases to adjudicate, the person expecting damages was not able to receive the compensation in time and due to the court fee, the victim was further discouraged to not file for compensation. This was remedied in 1988 Act where a separate court for motor accident claims was formed and without paying any ad-valorem court fee. In this act, licensing of the motorists and registration of the vehicle mandatory.

Further, it made it mandatory to obtain a Learner's license for all the drivers wanting to get a license and it was made obligatory to use the L board and the company of an instructor while driving in a public place. It also proposed that any person under the age of 20 is not allowed to drive a vehicle in a public place and a learner's license or driving license should only be issued if he or she is qualified.

This act was further substituted by Motor Vehicle (Amendment) Act of 2019 whose aim was to ensure road safety and stricter rules. The notable features of this Act encompass damages up to two lakhs for road accident victims and hefty fines for wilful offenders. The bill also mentions a recall of those vehicles which entail undue safety risks to other motorists, the driver, and the environment. With the amendment of the bill, the Central government created the National Road Safety Board as an advisory board to manage and regulate road safety and traffic.

What is Claims Tribunal?

Established by Motor Vehicle Act 1988, Claims Tribunal is defined under Chapter XII in Section 165 which authorises the State Government to constitute Claims Tribunals to adjudicate on the claims for compensation which emerge from motor vehicle accidents, ensuing death or bodily injury to persons or damage to any property of third parties. Its objective is to provide remedy to the victims of accident by motor vehicles in appropriate time without any procrastination. Motor Accident Claims Tribunals [MACT

Courts] handle those claims which are in relation to loss of life/property or those injury cases arising out of Motor Accidents.

These Claims need to be directly filed in the respective Tribunal. MACT Courts are administered by Judicial Officers from Delhi Higher Judicial Service. Currently these Courts are under immediate supervision of the High Courts of various States. Under Section 165 (2) the number of members to be assigned in Claims Tribunal is more than/equal to two, one of them is to nominated as the Chairman and under Section 165 (3), the eligibility for the appointment of members is that the member should be a Judge of a High Court or District Judge or ought to be eligible for appointment as a Judge of a High Court or District Judge.

How to obtain a driving license in India?

Driving Licence

To drive two-wheeler or four-wheeler legally on the roads, an Indian driving licence is mandatory. However, a permanent driving license cannot be received right away. There is a separate process for it.

An individual who wants to drive any type of motor vehicle in India has to get his/her learner's license first. A learner's license is issued for learning. After a month of the issued learner's license, the person has to appear for the test in front of an RTO authority, who upon proper examination, will declare if he/she has passed the exam or not.

Types of DL in India

There are three different types of licences issued in India:

- Learner's licence
- Permanent licence
- Commercial Driving Licence

- **Learner's licence:**

  - The Road Transport Authority (RTA) issues a learner's licence to the applicant before giving a permanent driving licence. It is valid for up to 6 months.
  - To get this licence, the applicant needs to submit valid documents at the RTO and pass a small test.
  - During the period of six months, the applicant is expected to polish his driving skills.
  - If the applicant still does not feel confident about driving, he can extend his learning licence.

- **Permanent licence:**

  - The RTA issues a permanent driving licence post the completion learner's licence period if the applicant meets the eligibility criteria.
  - As per the criteria, the applicant should be 18 years of age and should clear the driving test.
  - In case he fails the driving test, he can reappear for it after seven days of time.

- **Commercial driving licence:**

  - This commercial driving licence is specifically issued to heavy vehicle drivers such as trucks and delivery vans.
  - The criteria for this are that the applicant should be 18 years of age or above (some states also keep 20 years as minimum age), should be trained either in a

government training centre or a government-affiliated centre, should have completed education till 8th grade, has valid documents and already possess a learner's licence.

Eligibility Criteria for Driving Licence in India

i. Vehicles without gears with engine capacity up to 50cc =16 years of age and parental consent.
v. Vehicle with gears = 18 Years of age
v. Commercial Vehicle = 20 year of age ,

Document Required for Driving Licence

To ensure that there is no delay in the application process, the documents that are to be submitted have to be valid and correct. The list of documents required for driving licence are as follows:

Age Proof (any one of the below given documents)

- Birth Certificate
- PAN Card
- Passport
- 10th Class mark sheet
- Transfer certificate from any school for any class with date of birth printed on it.

Proof of Address required for DL:

Permanent Proof of address (any one from the following):

- Passport
- Aadhaar Card
- Self-owned house agreement

- Electricity bill (issued in applicants name)
- LIC bond
- Voters ID Card
- Ration Card

Current Proof of address (any one from the following):

- Rental agreement and electricity bill
- Rental agreement and LPG bill

Other Requirements for Driving Licence:

- Duly filled application form (to get the application form for driving licence, visit the nearest RTO or download it from the online portal for your state)
- 6 passport sized photographs (when applying for Learners Licence)
- 1 passport sized photograph (when applying for Driving Licence)
- Application Fees.
- If you are staying in other cities, as current address proof, you can present the rental agreement with one recent utility bill copy which can be a gas bill or electric bill.
- Medical Certificate - Form 1 A and 1 which is to be issued by a certified Government doctor.
- For all applicants over the age of 40 years, a medical certificate is mandatory.

How to Apply for Driving Licence (DL)

You can apply for DL either through the official government website or by visiting the nearest RTO office. But do note that having a learner's licence is a prerequisite for a driving licence application. Other than that, the applicant must be of or above 18 years of age and have knowledge of traffic rules and regulations to be eligible for the licence.

How to Check the Driving Licence Status?

To check the driving licence status online, follow the steps mentioned below:

Step 1: On the main page, click on the "Online Services" tab.

Step 2: From the drop-down menu, click on the "Driving Licence Related Services" tab.

Step 3: Select the state in which you have applied for a driving licence, from the drop-down menu.

Step 4: Click on the "Application Status" tab present at the top-right.

Step 5: Enter the details required like, "Application Number", "Date of Birth", and "Captcha".

Step 6: Click on "Submit".

CHAPTER SEVENTEEN

Environment

Environment means anything that surrounds us. It can be living (biotic) or non-living (abiotic) things. It includes physical, chemical and other natural forces. Living things live in their environment. They constantly interact with it and adapt themselves to conditions in their environment. In the environment there are different interactions between animals, plants, soil, water, and other living and non-living things.

Since everything is part of the environment of something else, the word environment is used to talk about many things. People in different fields of knowledge use the word environment differently. Electromagnetic environment is radio waves and other electromagnetic radiation and magnetic fields. The environment of galaxy refers to conditions of interstellar medium.

In psychology and medicine, a person's environment is the people, physical things and places that the person lives with. The environment affects the growth and development of the person. It affects the person's behavior, body, mind and heart.

The living conditions of living organisms in an environment are affected by the weather or climate changes in the environment.

Environment Protection Act, 1986

Environment Protection Act, 1986 Act of the Parliament of India. In the wake of the Bhopal gas Tragedy or Bhopal Disaster, the [Government of India] enacted the Environment Protection Act of 1986 under Article 253 of the Constitution. Passed in May 1986, it came into force on 19 November 1986. It has 26 sections and 4 chapters. The purpose of the Act is to implement the decisions of the United Nations Conference on the Human Environment. They relate to the protection and improvement of the human environment and the prevention of hazards to human beings, other living creatures, plants and property. The Act is an "umbrella" legislation designed to provide a framework for central government coordination of the activities of various central and state authorities established under previous laws, such as the Water Act and the Air Act.

History

This act was enacted by the Parliament of India in 1986. As the introduction says, "An Act to provide for the protection and improvement of environment and for matters connected therewith: Where as the decisions were taken at the United Nations Conference on the Human Environment held at Stockholm in June, 1972, in which India participated, to take appropriate steps for the protection and improvement of human environment. Where as it is considered necessary further to implement the decisions aforesaid in so far as they relate to the protection and improvement of environment and the prevention of hazards to human beings, other living creatures, plants and property". [2] This was due to Bhopal Gas Tragedy which was considered as the worst industrial tragedy in India.

Sections for environment protection act

This act has four Chapters and 26 Sections.

Chapter one consists of Preliminary information such as Short Title, Extend, Date of Commencement and Definitions. The definitions are given in the second section of the Act. Chapter two describes general powers of Central Government. Chapter 3 gives the Central Government the power to take action to protect the environment. Chapter 4 allows government to appoint officers to achieve these objectives. It also gives the government the power to give direction to closure, prohibition or regulation of industry, pollution. The act has provisions for penalties for contravention of the provisions of the act and rules, orders and directions. It also gives detail if the offence is done by a company or government department. It says for such offence the in-charge and head of department respectively would be liable for punishment.

Outlines of different Indian laws on environment

There are certain constitutional provisions which give certain power and rights to the citizens to protect environment. Let's have a look:

Article 48A: This Article comes under the Directive principle of the State policy. This article implies that State shall endeavor to protect the environment. It also emphasizes on safeguarding the forests and wildlife of the country. Article 48A imposes a duty on State to protect the environment from pollution by adopting various measures.

Article 51A (g): The Article 51 A(g) states that it shall be the duty of each and every citizen of India to protect and improve the natural environment that includes lakes, rivers, forests and wildlife. This Article also focuses on showing compassion for living creatures. This article is similar to Article 48A, but the only difference is that it concentrates on fundamental duty of citizens whereas Article 48A instructs the state to perform their duties and protect environment. Hence, it is our duty to not only protect the environment from pollution but also improve its quality.

Article 253: This Article gives power to Parliament to create laws for the country in order to implement any treaty conventions and agreement with other countries. By this article, Parliament enacted various laws in order to protect environment like - Water Act 1974, Air Act 1981 and the Environmental Protection Act 1984.

Article 246: The Article 246 divides the subjects of legislation between Union and State. It also provides the details of Concurrent list in which both the Union and State make laws by sharing the jurisdiction comprising the protection of mines, wildlife and minerals development. So, both State and Union have power to enact laws to protect the environment. Article 246 also provides the extra power to Parliament in order to make laws in State list for the National interest.

Article 47: This article imposes duty on the State in order to improve the standards of living of citizens by providing health facilities, proper nutrition, and sanitization and protect the environment to live safely. Article 47 also pressurizes its citizens to be more conscious of the environment.

Article 21: It states that right to life is not just for animals but it also provides the right to humans to live safely in an environment with basic human dignities. Because. In M.C. Mehta vs. Union of India, Supreme Court had stated that the right to live includes living in a pollution-free environment and be free from diseases.

Article 19(1) (g): It states that citizens cannot practice such trade or business activities which are hazardous to public health.

Article 32 & 226: This article provides right to citizen to approach to Supreme or High Court whenever there is violation of fundamental right by PIL (Public Interest Litigation). This article helps preserve the environment and maintain ecological balance. This Article also dictates that environment conservation is not just the duty of government but also the responsibility of citizens of India.

Environmental Laws in India after Independence (1947)

The Indian Constitution adopted in 1950 never dealt with the subject of environment or prevention until 1976 amendment was not passed. The post independent Indian approach was centered on the economic development and poverty alleviation.

Let's look at some of the progressive steps in context of environmental laws in India after independence:

- It was the Stockholm Declaration of 1972 that turned the attention of the Indian Government towards the perspective of environmental protection.

- Set up in 1972, the National Council for Environmental Policy and Planning was later evolved into Ministry of Environment and Forests (MoEF) in 1985.
- The Wildlife Protection Act 1972 aims at rational and modern wildlife management.
- The Water (Prevention and Control of Pollution) Act, 1974 provides the establishment of pollution control boards both at Centre and States in order to act as watchdogs for preventing and controlling pollution.
- The Air (Prevention and Control of Pollution) Act 1981, aims at checking air pollution via pollution control boards.
- The Forest (Conservation) Act 1980, aims at checking deforestation and diversion of forest land.
- The Public Liability Insurance Act, 1991 provides mandatory insurance to provide immediate relief to the person affected by accidents while handling any hazardous substance.
- The Biological Diversity Act 2002 safeguards the threatened species, prevents bio - piracy and water scarcity. It also regularizes the usage of natural resources and avoid its over exhaustion
- It was the Stockholm Declaration of 1972 that turned the attention of the Indian Government towards the perspective of environmental protection.
- Set up in 1972, the National Council for Environmental Policy and Planning was later evolved into Ministry of Environment and Forests (MoEF) in 1985.
- The Wildlife Protection Act 1972 aims at rational and modern wildlife management.
- The Water (Prevention and Control of Pollution) Act, 1974 provides the establishment of pollution control boards both at Centre and States in order to act as

watchdogs for preventing and controlling pollution.

- The Air (Prevention and Control of Pollution) Act 1981, aims at checking air pollution via pollution control boards.
- The Forest (Conservation) Act 1980, aims at checking deforestation and diversion of forest land.
- The Public Liability Insurance Act, 1991 provides mandatory insurance to provide immediate relief to the person affected by accidents while handling any hazardous substance.
- The Biological Diversity Act 2002 safeguards the threatened species, prevents bio - piracy and water scarcity. It also regularizes the usage of natural resources and avoid its over exhaustion

CHAPTER EIGHTEEN

Indian labour law

Indian labour law refers to law regulating labour in India. Traditionally, Indian government at federal and state level have sought to ensure a high degree of protection for workers, but in practice, this differs due to form of government and because labour is a subject in the concurrent list of the Indian Constitution.

Constitutional rights

In the Constitution of India from 1950, articles 14-16, 19(1)(c), 23-24, 38, and 41-43A directly concern labour rights. Article 14 states everyone should be equal before the law, article 15 specifically says the state should not discriminate against citizens, and article 16 extends a right of "equality of opportunity" for employment or appointment under the state. Article 19(1)(c) gives everyone a specific right "to form associations or unions". Article 23 prohibits all trafficking and forced labour, while article 24 prohibits child labour under 14 years old in a factory, mine or "any other hazardous employment".

Articles 38-39, and 41-43A, however, like all rights listed in Part IV of the Constitution are not enforceable by courts, rather than creating an aspirational "duty of the

State to apply these principles in making laws".[4] The original justification for leaving such principles unenforceable by the courts was that democratically accountable institutions ought to be left with discretion, given the demands they could create on the state for funding from general taxation, although such views have since become controversial. Article 38(1) says that in general the state should "strive to promote the welfare of the people" with a "social order in which justice, social, economic and political, shall inform all the institutions of national life. In article 38(2) it goes on to say the state should "minimise the inequalities in income" and based on all other statuses. Article 41 creates a "right to work", which the National Rural Employment Guarantee Act 2005 attempts to put into practice. Article 42 requires the state to "make provision for securing just and human conditions of work and for maternity relief". Article 43 says workers should have the right to a living wage and "conditions of work ensuring a decent standard of life". Article 43A, inserted by the Forty-second Amendment of the Constitution of India in 1976,[5] creates a constitutional right to codetermination by requiring the state to legislate to "secure the participation of workers in the management of undertakings".

Workmen's Compensation Act,1923

The workmen's compensation act, 1923, is a type of social security legislation that was enacted to make the employer liable for paying the compensation to its employees who got effected or to their dependents in case of demise. The compensation is paid in event of an accident or injury (including some occupational disease) that arises out of or during the employment and that results in total or partial disablement or demise of the worker.

The compensation act for workmen was formed after it came into notice that the laborers were becoming exposed to the danger by using more sophisticated and advanced machinery. According to the compensation act of 1884, the employer would take responsibility for the compensation of its workmen only when some major or fatal accidents occur on road. However, in 1885, the mining and factory inspectors realized that this Fatal Act, 1885, is not sufficient.

The Government gave it a hearing ear, when the Legislative Assembly members, representatives of employer, experts in medicine, workers, and insurance experts formed a committee that provided a report that led to the Workmen's Compensation Act, 1923.

When this act was passed, it put a stop and provided relief to the workers who would have gone through the processing of court that is generally expensive. It was an effort to seek compensation whenever they encounter some injury during employment.

Scope of Workmen's Compensation Act

The workmen's compensation act, 1923, is applicable for those workers who are working with an industry that is mentioned in the act. Under this act, the protection of workmen from injuries and losses caused through an accident in course of and arising out of the employment subject to specific expectations as mentioned in the act.

The objective of the Workmen's Compensation Act

The Workmen's Compensation Act, 1923 was majorly formed to provide compensation to the workmen at the time of an accident.

The act mentions that it is the duty and responsibility of the employer to include the welfare of the workers when an injury is the result of the employment in the same way the employer has reserved the right of making profits. The main aim of this act is to ensure that the workmen have sustainable life even after encountering an employment-related injury.

The Liability of the Employer for Compensation

To make the employer pay the compensation at the time of injury or death suffered by the employee or workman should be a consequence of some accident in course of or out of his/her employment depends on the following four conditions:

- The causal connection between the accident and the injury (which is personal injury is caused to a workman while he/she is on work).
- The probability is based on the reason that work has contributed because of personal injury.
- The accident and injury that is caused during the employment course.
- The applicant who proves that the accident or injury occurred during work and its results strain that has aggravated or contributed to the injury.

Applicability of the Workmen's Compensation Act

This act is applicable across India except for Jammu and Kashmir. This act does not apply to the areas that are covered by the Employees State Insurance Act, 1948.

The Rules for Workmen's Compensation Have Changed in 2020

There is good news for the workers as the Central Government has changed the rules for the calculation of the compensation of the employees under the Workmen's Compensation Act, 1923. The notification for the same has sent on 3rd January 2020 in which the amount of the wages, which were considered previously for compensation's calculation was Rs.8, 000, are now increased to Rs.15, 000 as per the Ministry of Labour and Employment.

Since 2010, the Workmen's Compensation Act, 1923 was known as the Employee's Compensation Act. It offers compensation to the employees who suffer or die total or partial disablement because of an accident while on work. The compensation is paid by the employer and an employee who is eligible to get compensation from ESIC cannot claim compensation under the Employee's Compensation Act, 1923.

Conditions When Employer is Not Liable to Pay Compensation

According to the workmen's compensation act, an employer has to pay the compensation to its employee when he/she encounters some personal injury due to an accident that arose during an employee's employment. An employer is not liable for paying the compensation if:

- An injury that doesn't result in partial or total disablement of the employee for more than three days.
- Any injury that does not result in permanent total disability or death because of an accident in the influence of drugs or drink.
- If an employee meets with an accident that is caused because of wilful disobedience of the rules by him/her and wilful safety guard removal.

Calculation of the Compensation

The calculation of compensation as per the act is performed according to the provisions under Section four of the Workmen's Compensation Act:

- **In Case of an Accident that Results in Permanent Total Disablement:** In this case, an amount equal to 60% of injured employee's monthly wage into the relevant factor or Rs.1, 20, 000, whichever is more is given.
- **When an Accident Results in Death:** An amount that is equal to 50% of the monthly wage of the deceased employee into the relevant factor or an amount equal to Rs.1, 20, 000, whichever is more

The Final Words:

The Workmen's Compensation Act, 1923 was made to offer compensation to the workers who have encountered injuries due to an accident during their employment. This act ensures that rights of the laborers are maintained even after they encounter some disability or death due to an accident during their work. Therefore, the employers are obligated to offer compensation to their workers who encountered injuries that have led to demise or disablement during employment.

Trade Unions Act, 1926

The primary function of the Trade Unions Act was to protect the interests of workers against discrimination and unfair labor practice and also provide them a blanket cover to stand up for their interests through the formation of trade unions. Through this article, the rights and regulations of the Trade unions Act have been covered including the scope and objectives of the act.

The trade Unions Act, 1926 provides for registration of trade unions with a view to render lawful organisation of labour to enable collective bargaining. It also confers on a registered trade union certain protection and privileges.

The Act extends to the whole of India and applies to all kinds of unions of workers and associations of employers, which aim at regularising labour management relations. A Trade Union is a combination whether temporary or permanent, formed for regulating the relations not only between workmen and employers but also between workmen and workmen or between employers and employers.

Objectives & Scope of Trade Unions Act, 1926:

- **Ensure Security of Workers:**

This ensured continued employment of workers, prevent retrenchment, lay off or lock-outs. Controlled application of â€œfireâ€? or dismissal or discharge and VRS.

- **Obtain Better Economic Returns:**

This ensured wages hike at periodic intervals, bonus at higher rate, other admissible allowances, subsidized canteen and transport facilities.

- **Secure Power To Influence Management:**

This ensured workersâ€™ participation in management, decision making, role of union in policy decisions affecting workers, and staff members.

- **Secure Power To Influence Government:**

This ensured influence on government to pass labour legislation which improves working conditions, safety, welfare, security and retirement benefits of workers and their dependents, seek redressal of grievances as and when needed.

Functions of a Trade Union:

- To secure fair wages to workers.To safeguard security of tenure and improve conditions of service.
- To enlarge opportunities for promotion and training
- To improve working and living conditions.

- To provide for educational, cultural and recreational facilities.
- To co-operate in and facilitate technological advance by broadening the understanding of workers on its underlying issues.
- To promote identity of interests of workers with their industry.
- To offer responsive co-operation in improving levels of production and productivity, discipline and high standards of quality and
- To promote individual and collective welfare.

Payment of Wages Act, 1936

The Payment of Wages Act, 1936 regulates payment of wages to employees (direct and indirect). The act is intended to be a remedy against unauthorized deductions made by employer and/or unjustified delay in payment of wages.

Regular Pay

Payment should be made before the 7th day of a month where the number of workers is less than 1000 and 10th day otherwise. The wage-period shall not exceed 1 month. The Act is applicable only to employees drawing wages not exceeding Rs. 6500 a month.

Mode of Payment

Under the act, payment has to be made in currency notes or coins. Cheque payment or crediting to bank account is allowed with consent in writing by the employee. (Section 6)

Deduction from Wages

Employer is allowed to effect only authorized deductions, as specified in the Act. This include fines (Section 8), absence from duty (Section 9), Damages or loss (Section 10), deduction for services (amenities) given to employer (Section 11) recovery of advances and loans (Section 12, 13) and payment to cooperative society and insurance (Section 13).

Claims for excessive deduction and Non Payment

Employers individually or through trade union can approach the authority (Labour Office) for relief. (Section 15, 16, 17)

Minimum Wages Act 1948

The **Minimum Wages Act 1948** is an Act of Parliament concerning Indian labour law that sets the minimum wages that must be paid to skilled and unskilled labours.

The Indian Constitution has defined a 'living wage' that is the level of income for a worker which will ensure a basic standard of living including good health, dignity, comfort, education and provide for any contingency. However, to keep in mind an industry's capacity to pay the constitution has defined a 'fair wage'.[1] Fair wage is that level of wage that not just maintains a level of employment, but seeks to increase it keeping in perspective the industry's capacity to pay. Due to an unjust attention towards the decades old law it is now exploited by major businesses to underpay their employees, In public opinion government must set an yearly wage change just like countries internationally do.

To achieve this in its first session during November 1948, the Central Advisory Council appointed a Tripartite

Committee of Fair Wage. This committee came up with the concept of a minimum wage, which not only guarantees bare subsistence and preserves efficiency but also provides for education, medical requirements and some level of comfort.[1]

India introduced the Minimum Wages Act in 1948,[2] giving both the Central government and State government jurisdiction in fixing wages. The act is legally non-binding, but statutory. Payment of wages below the minimum wage rate amounts to forced labour. Wage boards are set up to review the industry's capacity to pay and fix minimum wages such that they at least cover a family of four's requirements of calories, shelter, clothing, education, medical assistance, and entertainment. Under the law, wage rates in scheduled employments differ across states, sectors, skills, regions and occupations owing to difference in costs of living, regional industries' capacity to pay, consumption patterns, etc. Hence, there is no single uniform minimum wage rate across the country and the structure has become overly complex. The highest minimum wage rate as updated in 2012 was Rs. 322/day in Andaman and Nicobar[3] and the lowest was Rs. 38/day in Tripura.[4] In Mumbai, as of 2017, the minimum wage was Rs. 348/day for a *safai karmachari* (sewage cleaner and sweeper), but this was rarely paid.

Contents

The Act provides for fixing wage rate (time, piece, guaranteed time, overtime) for any industry .

1) While fixing hours for a normal working day as per the act should make sure of the following:

- The number of hours that are to be fixed for a normal working day should have one or more intervals/breaks included.
- At least one day off from an entire week should be given to the employee for rest.
- Payment for the day decided to be given for rest should be paid at a rate not less than the overtime rate.

2) If an employee is involved in work that categorises his service in two or more scheduled employments, the employee's wage will include respective wage rate of all work for the number of hours dedicated at each task.

3) It is mandatory for the employer to maintain records of all employee's work, wages and receipts .

4) Appropriate governments will define and assign the task of inspection and appoint inspectors for the same.

Equal Remuneration Act

The Equal Remuneration Act, 1976 provides for payment of equal remuneration to men and women and help prevent gender discrimination. Article 39 of the Indian Constitution envisages that the States will have a policy for securing equal pay for equal work for both men and women. To give effect to these constitutional provisions, the Equal Remuneration Act, 1976 was introduced.

Duties of Employer

Under the Equal Remuneration Act, employers require to ensure the following to workmen:

- No employer shall pay to any worker, employed by him in an establishment or employment, remuneration, whether payable in cash or in-kind, at rates less favourable than those at which he pays remuneration to the workers of the opposite sex in such establishment or employment for performing the same work or work of a similar nature.
- No employer to comply with the Equal Remuneration Act can reduce the rate or salary of any worker.

Also, no employer while making recruitment for the same work or work of a similar nature can make any discrimination against women except where the employment of women in such work is prohibited or restricted by a law in force.

Maintenance of Register

All employers require to maintain a register and other documents about the workers employed as per the prescribed rules. Rule 6 of the Equal Remunerations Rules provides that every employer maintain a register about the workers employed by him in Form D.

Penalty under the Equal Remuneration Act

The penalty under the Equal Remuneration Act separate into two categories as follows:

Minor Infraction

If an employer commits any of the following offences under the Equal Remuneration Act, a penalty of Rs.1000 can be levied.

- Omits or fails to maintain any register or document about workers employed.
- Omits or fails to produce any register, muster-roll or other document about the employment of workers.
- Omits or refuses to give any evidence or prevents his agent, servant or any other person in charge of the establishment, or any worker, from giving evidence.

Major Infraction

If an employer commits any of the following offences under the Equal Remuneration Act, a penalty of Rs.5000 can be levied.

- Discriminates in recruitment in contravention to the Equal Remuneration Act.
- Makes a payment of remuneration at unequal rates to men and women workers, for the same work or work of a similar nature.
- Makes any discrimination between men and women workers in contravention of the Equal Remuneration Act.
- Omits or fails to carry out any direction made by the Government.

In case any of the offences are committed by a Company, every person who, at the time of the offence committed was in charge of and was responsible to the company, for the conduct of the business will be deemed to be guilty of the offence and will be liable to be proceeded and punished accordingly.

Maternity Benefit (Amendment) Act, 2017

The Maternity (Amendment) Bill 2017, an amendment to the Maternity Benefit Act, 1961, was passed in Rajya Sabha on 11 August 2016, in Lok Sabha on 9 March 2017, and received an assent from President of India on 27 March 2017.[2] The Maternity Benefit Act, 1961 protects the employment of women during the time of her maternity and entitles her of a 'maternity benefit' – i.e. full paid absence from work – to take care for her child. The Act is applicable to all establishments employing 10 or more than 10 persons in Factories, Mines, Plantation, Shops & Establishments and other entities.[3] Establishments employing 50 or more employees are also required to provide crèche facilities, either separately or along with common facilities within a prescribed distance.[4]

The provisions of this act are effective from 1 April 2017. However, provision on creche facility (Section 11A) shall be effective from 1 July 2017. The Code on Social Security, 2020 consolidated the provisions of this and several other acts, repealing the acts in the process.

Applicability

The Act was applicable to all establishments which include factories, mines, plantations, Government establishments, shops and establishments under the relevant applicable legislation, or any other establishment as may be notified by the Central Government

Eligibility

As per the Act, to be eligible for maternity benefit, a woman must have been working as an employee in an establishment for a period of at least 80 days within the past 12 months. Payment during the leave period is based on the average daily wage for the period of actual absence

Key amendments

- **Increased Paid Maternity Leave:**

The Maternity Benefit Amendment Act has increased the duration of paid maternity leave available for women employees from the existing 12 weeks to 26 weeks. Under the Maternity Benefit Amendment Act, this benefit could be availed by women for a period extending up to a maximum of 8 weeks before the expected delivery date and the remaining time can be availed after childbirth. For women who are having 2 or more surviving children, the duration of paid maternity leave shall be 12 weeks (i.e. 6 weeks before and 6 weeks after expected date of delivery).

- **Maternity leave for adoptive and commissioning mothers:**

Maternity leave of 12 weeks to be available to mothers adopting a child below the age of three months from the date of adoption as well as to the "commissioning mothers". The commissioning mother has been defined as biological mother who uses her egg to create an embryo planted in any other woman.

- **Work from Home option:**

The Maternity Benefit Amendment Act has also introduced an enabling provision relating to "work from home" for women, which may be exercised after the expiry of the 26 weeks' leave period. Depending upon the nature of work, women employees may be able to avail this benefit on terms that are mutually agreed with the employer.

- **Creche facility:**

The Maternity Benefit Amendment Act makes creche facility mandatory for every establishment employing 50 or more employees. Women employees would be permitted to visit the crèche 4 times during the day (including rest intervals)

The Maternity Benefit Amendment Act makes it mandatory for employers to educate women about the maternity benefits available to them at the time of their appointment.

Criticism

- **Gender discrimination against women having childbearing age:**

Policy design is important and making such leave an employer mandate, as in India, ensures employers will discriminate against women of childbearing age. Additional requirements like creche facilities require more capital and operating expenditure. It won't come as a surprise that some companies in India might shy away from hiring young women. When they do, the women might face a reduction in compensation as firms compensate for higher lifetime costs.

- **Types of burden on the employer:**

Employers have to bear the entire cost of providing leave to employees—in terms of both continued pay while on leave, as well as the indirect cost of having to get the work done by employing other workers to finish the work of the absent employee. Also, it increases the cost of temporary training provided to the employee which is employed on behalf of the absent employee.

- **Women will lose their jobs:**

Regarding how the bulk of employment is in the informal sector, Team-lease estimates, that 11-18 Lakh jobs for women will be lost because of the implementation of the Act, over the first four years.

- **Financial burden only on employer:**

In most countries, the cost of maternity leave is shared by the government, employer, insurance agency and other social security programs. In Singapore, for example, the employer bears the cost for 8 weeks and public funds for 8 weeks. In Australia and Canada, public funds bear the full cost. A social insurance scheme bears the cost in France. In Brazil, it shared by the employer, employee and the government.

https://annusehrawat8520.blogspot.com/

www.ingramcontent.com/pod-product-compliance
Ingram Content Group UK Ltd.
Pitfield, Milton Keynes, MK11 3LW, UK
UKHW041957190726
13854UKWH00005B/2026

9 798885 466370